D1502126

Unmute Yourself, Girlfriend

A CLASS ACT
a Zoom through the Pandemic at Seventy

A MEMOIR ANTHOLOGY
EDITED BY Susan Dukow

Published by BookBaby.com

2021

Contents

Foreword
by Oren Whyche-Shaw

IN MARCH 2020, THE ENTIRE WORLD WAS CONFRONTED with the frightening COVID-19 pandemic. The magnitude, rate of infections, and number of deaths – more than a half million – have been overwhelming. All citizens of the globe have been impacted by this scourge and in their own way, adjusted to quarantine and, in some cases, isolation. The main focus for all has been to survive and thrive, not only for themselves but also for their families and communities. In addition to COVID, the last year has seen extreme political polarization within the United States. What were accepted norms of behavior for political leadership as well as the citizenry have been thrown asunder, leaving the unanswered question of "where do we go from here?" The challenges of living in the last twelve months have been daunting.

This is a collection of essays written by forty-three women who graduated from the Philadelphia High School for Girls in 1968. They were known as "the 212th Class" then and are now considered "senior citizens." They have all lived and garnered experience and wisdom since leaving Girls' High as their writings reveal. Some of the stories focus principally on the impact of COVID on their lives. Others tell how attending the Philadelphia High School for Girls, and reconnecting with their classmates forty or fifty years later, has helped them to find the strength to withstand their changing lives as well as recent events. And, there are accounts that reflect on much broader themes. The essays are diverse and based upon the individual lives lived but all are relatable. I know I could relate to many of them and I think you, the reader, will too. Most importantly, I hope this book makes you reflect on your own resilience, and the challenges and successes you've had in your life.

It is an honor to have been asked to write this Foreword. As an alumna who graduated a year earlier than these women, reading these stories brings back those long-ago high school experiences and the friendships established. I believe this collection is a true reflection of the "Intangible Spirit" of every Girls' High girl.

Enjoy!

Oren Whyche-Shaw
Distinguished Daughter, Philadelphia High School for Girls
The 211th Class
Herald Harbor on the Severn, MD
March 2021

Preface
by Janice Miller Abrams

ON JUNE 13, 1968, THE 212TH CLASS OF THE PHILADEL-
phia High School for Girls graduated and entered the world, each of us
with our own hopes, dreams, ambitions, and realities. Over the course
of the next five decades, we lived those lives, going our separate ways,
experiencing triumph and tragedy, joy and pain.

Through reunions, chat groups, and social media we came back
together. It was a time to see old friends and to reminisce, to reconnect,
and to remember those we had lost. But most of all it was the beginning
of a conversation.

Unmute Yourself, Girlfriend is the continuation of those exchanges.
We each came of age at a moment of profound change in our country and
are all living today through another inflection point. This book is not an ideal-
ized version of a shared history but rather a series of individual perspectives.
The contributions to this collection unveil not only common threads but also
vastly different experiences and viewpoints. The idea behind this project was
to create a somewhat pointillist portrait of a half century lived. Some stories
are wide ranging, others narrow. All are personal. The picture that emerges
is rich and revealing. Though we have shared the same times, our individual
journeys are unique.

These are our stories.

Austin, TX
March 2021

Acknowledgements

TO ALL FORTY-THREE OF OUR WRITERS WHO SHARED
their individual stories and most especially for playing well together and
making this project sheer joy.

Our heartfelt thanks to our proofreading teams, Marsha Kramer
Prosini and Fran Nachman, our fearless first-rounders, and Patricia Anne
McDonnell, Sharon Ozlek Dunoff, Jane Pearl Barr and Ruth Stark who
brought up the rear. All who worked tirelessly with humor and consider-
able effort every single time a comma or semicolon debate ensued. Our
very own Grammar Police were in the house!

After preserving Sherrie Harabin's story in a safe place for over five
decades, Nona Safra composed one of her own as a loving dedication.
Janice Miller Abrams penned an eloquent Preface for our book.

A good-natured husband and professional photographer, Rich
Dunoff helped us salvage old images and remarked that it was the first
time someone of our age and gender asked him to please show aging
and all the wrinkles.

We especially thank Oren Whyche-Shaw for writing the Foreword
after meeting us only once during the first annual Zoom 'Galentine'
Celebration, February 13th 2021, with the Girls' High Alumnae
Association.

And last but not least, we embrace the Philadelphia High School for
Girls Alumnae Association for the encouraging and enthusiastic response
you have shown to our project. This one is for you - our labor of love!

To Work Or Not To Work,
Or
Perils of a Snowy Night

by Sherrie Harabin

Thousands stare glassy-eyed at the quickly drifting snow. "I think the flakes ARE GETTING BIGGER," one voice ventures.

Thousands of minds feel the rumblings of brain erosion because of overdoses of everything from "Fundamentos de Español" to ionizing a dilute solution of sulphuric acid.

Thousands of hands flip the covers of textbooks to a frustrated close. Somewhere a sleepy voice mumbles, ". . . probably won't have school tomorrow, anyhow. At least I *hope* not. Gads, I haven't finished history yet!"

And so those thousands of eyes, minds, and hands group themselves into sets of threes; the effort is just too much.

Flick. In desperation radios are switched on.

". . . So get those announcements to CBB, care of WIBG." (Two second pause and then a sudden barrage of jungle music.) "Hey, gang, talking about the swingingest place in Philly town — St. Alice's. Now this Saturday . . ."

"All right, yes, yes," the countless number of home swingers repeat to themselves, "sure, *this* Saturday — St. Alice's — but, please, just give the school closings?"

"This is Hy Ski McVaddio Zoot, your man with the plan for the greater sounds in life. Sol-lid! Well, pardner, just got in word about school closings and the word is — the word is, concerning public and parochial schools, that there is no word just yet, but there will be at 5:30 tomorrow morning. So you just . . ."

CLICK.

So maybe it is about 9:00 p.m. or somewhere around then. What can these red-blooded, healthy, all-American Philadelphians do until the word is given? They can return to their books and forget about snow *or* they can return to their books, forget about the snow but just get up every four minutes for a drink of water and a peek out the bathroom window, *OR* they can get out their binoculars, pull up all the shades, turn out the lights, and keep a close count with a millimeter stick. But then again, there are others who go to bed.

Upon waking, the student gropes for the radio only to be greeted by a bombastic blast of "When you smi-le . . ." Battling the urge to close their eyes, they grimace through several commercials when guilt creeps over them because of the uncompleted history. The tension is almost more than they can bear; there is no nail polish left on their fingers when suddenly like the blast of a bugle: "All public and parochial, we repeat for the sake of those who missed the previous announcement, (sadistic radio announcer!) all public and parochial schools are (pause) closed."

A thousand sighs, a thousand cheers, a thousand snores . . .

In Loving Memory of

SHERRIE HARABIN

… and to all our other classmates who have passed too soon, these stories are dedicated to you in honor of our sisterhood then and now.

Dedication by Nona Safra

THE 212 HAS BEEN A CLASS WITH WRITERS – FOR SOME of us, the words flow like the rapids in the rivers of our beloved state of Pennsylvania while for others, they trickle like the streams we played in as young children and for a group of us, they sprout up periodically like dancing fountains on the Parkway. But, we all have our own individual unique stories, each of them like irreplaceable fibers that, together, form a tapestry of the women who we have become. In some ways, collecting these stories brings to mind that we have created a verbal version of the story quilts that are so treasured in American history.

Some of us took a first tentative step into having our work 'published' in the Iris leaflet while we were at Girls' High. So, it seems appropriate to start with a piece that was written by a classmate who is not here to write about reflections looking back from her seventieth year, the late Sherrie Harabin, who was lost to us in her sixteenth year.

For some reason, I saved *To Work or Not to Work* as a reminder that, though we were all very different, we shared some of the same experiences. As I read it now, it is clear that while we each shared a memory waiting to hear about school closures, we weren't all listening to the same radio station to hear the news - so, even in small ways, during our recollections and years together, we were on different frequencies.

Fifty-five years later, the same can be true - we are living through the same national and international events, each of us with a distinctive and different experience.

To all of our sisters who share their beautiful threads and help to weave the rich tapestry of the 212, thank you for showing how our lives have enriched us and helped bring light to the world!

Homer, AK
January 2021

Pauline Miriam Braverman

HOW I WOKE UP AT GHS

I ATTENDED GIRLS' HIGH FROM 1964 THROUGH 1968.
As a teenager, I was less involved with the academic training that was provided, and more involved in socializing with friends. GHS was quite unimportant to me. It was friends first and academia second.

As a direct result of the annoyance I felt attending school, my commitment to GHS was minimal. Added to this, I found my classmates to be more monied, very cliquish, better dressed, less friendly and possibly more committed to academia. I felt myself to be a part of a wheel turning that was not a reflection of me.

At age twelve I joined B'nai B'rith Girls (BBG). I began to learn leadership skills and devoted myself almost entirely to working within the organization until graduation. I excelled as a local and district (three states) leader. I was popular and always had a crowd around me. I always felt included. I was a happy teen. I led with a happy heart.

However, there were two events during my senior year at GHS that had a profound effect on me and contributed directly to my being "woke". For this, I am eternally grateful to my otherwise difficult academic years. All of us at Girls' High had these same experiences. My reaction began my wake-up call.

The first. In early April of every year, I would get excited because my birthday fell on April 10 and most teenagers love our birthdays. On April 4, 1968, the United States lost an iconic civil rights leader, Martin Luther King, Jr. I was heavily impacted emotionally. Not yet understanding how this event influenced our political system, I simply cried in shame for the unkindness of humanity. I didn't know why. I didn't understand any of it. All I knew was this was very wrong and against all tenants of kindness and love.

In early June, 1968, the class of 212 was preparing for graduation services. We were lining up in correct formation, walking down the aisles in our study hall when an announcement came over the loudspeaker. Robert F. Kennedy had been assassinated. I remember collapsing into the first seat I could find with tears in my eyes. Already living through the assassinations of both JFK and MLK, I felt overwhelmed with shame and sadness.

College students were beginning to march against the Vietnam War. Climate change was being addressed in a more casual way than it is today. Corporate greed was being looked at in a seriously different way. A cultural shift was in the air and I listened to its murmurs.

Even when walking down the aisle at graduation in my white dress and red rose, I felt the emergence of a new me. No longer satisfied with the status quo, I began to embrace a new ideology, very tenderly at first, but my eyes were opened for the first time.

The second. One day, again in my senior year, our principal and vice principal marched into my homeroom looking very stern and unyielding. They first spoke with my teacher and then left, taking one of my classmates with them. We were all shaken up because we didn't know what or why this was happening. As the day progressed, the rumors began. By the end of the day, we all knew that our classmate had possibly been expelled from school for having marijuana in her locker. Everyone was talking and making judgments about her, about marijuana, and about the newly evolving cultural values of the Boomers in the United States. On the eve of a cultural revolution, she was a victim of the establishment and I was appalled. We all had opinions that we openly expressed. My opinion and judgment were that although I never smoked marijuana, it was her right to do so. I placed no negative judgment upon her. I felt she had been victimized and what happened was so wrong. This was my big "woke". Graduation was upon us. I entered GHS naively but I graduated needing to understand the world around me.

It was 1968 and the counterculture movement was growing. I began marching in protest to the Vietnam War and, as I surrounded myself with open minded people, I became politically involved in "bucking the establishment". I thank GHS for helping to open my eyes.

Since graduation, I've been an activist. I protested the war, I believed in eating the rich, and I participated by "flyering" the halls of my college about the very first Earth Day being held on Belmont Plateau. As I worked alongside boys, I noted a huge discrepancy. The boys were making the rules even in our counterculture and the girls were used to distribute information. After being a BBG leader for so long, my organizational power was reduced because of my sex. In fact, I was being devalued because I was female. And I didn't like it.

I first heard the words "male chauvinist pig" while working with organizations against the "machine" and, although I was quick to agree, I had to use the dictionary to find the meaning of chauvinist. Believing that I should not be feeding into the goals of, or sleeping with the patriarchy, I came out in 1972 as a lesbian feminist separatist. Although I have released the separatist part of myself, I am still lesbian-centric and open-minded. I woke in 1968 when my classmate was busted. I believe this incident, along with the assassinations of our better politicians, opened my eye to a future that not many women have experienced. Thank you, GHS.

Since then, I've continued to be an activist, mostly as a second wave feminist. My resume is varied and full. I was a Lavender Menace (remember the NOW convention?), director of the Free Women's School for three semesters, on the editorial board of HERA, a feminist newspaper, a member of Dyketactics, involved in the SNUFF demonstrations, a working member of Resistance (Omega) Press (a radical print shop), the founder of Bad Girls Portland which has survived twenty-six years, and the founder of Hot Flash Dances for Women in Portland, Seattle, San Diego, and Phoenix.

I now live in the Pacific Northwest. The culture here is much, much different from South Philadelphia and Center City. I am seen as loud and too assertive. Without a family of my own (I never had children), it has gotten pretty lonely at sixty-nine. Having a 212 group to embrace, I can finally say that I am looking forward to connecting with my old classmates.

Vancouver, WA
Identifiable Portlander
January 2020

Paula Campbell

THE DIVINE GRACE OF 212
SISTERS IN THE AGE OF
THE COVID-19 PANDEMIC

IT'S CHRISTMAS SEASON IN THE YEAR 2020. IN THE state of California, we all received a statewide text to "Stay at Home" for we were in the midst of a second wave of the COVID-19 Pandemic. The current surge was actually predicted earlier in the year by epidemiologists. But since it was ridiculed by President Donald Trump there are maskless protests at our Capitol in Sacramento by angry citizens who are COVID-weary. Thousands want to impeach Governor Gavin Newsom for issuing new restrictions and forcing us to shelter in place again.

Nationally, half of America is anxiously awaiting the inauguration of President-Elect Joe Biden, hoping to return the nation to some normalcy after four years of the previous administration. The other half hopes the Republican Party will overturn the election for Trump based on his relentless false claims of election fraud. We stand at the crossroads of uncertainty as a result. There has been an unprecedented and violent attempt at a political coup in the United States of America. While, simultaneously, it is fair to say that sometimes ghastly thoughts emerge in the minds of Americans that the leadership responsible for allowing COVID to spread as a "hoax" are now profiting from its cure. The world looks on and has actually shuttered its doors to American Exceptionalism.

California's COVID-19 lockdown orders forced me to spend Christmas morning 2020 alone in my pajamas with a cup of Italian roast coffee. Though I routinely check-in to Facebook posts from 212 Sisters and friends ever since our fortieth GHS High School Reunion. Social media and technology have both been beneficial for me. I live off the grid in the mountains in the middle of a forest of Northern California. There I thrive in a white two-bedroom cottage with a flower trellis attached that overlooks ten acres of Dry Creek Canyon in Amador County. For the past twenty years I have been the only African American woman in my small, rural town of about three hundred other souls, give or take. I am seventy years old now. My hair is now white with long dreadlocks draping my shoulders that I had to wait until I retired to grow because of social norms. Ironically, a law was enacted in California last year banning discrimination of ethnic hair styles. But it came fifty years too late for me.

My family members who still have deep roots in the suburbs of Pennsylvania perceive my existence as rather eccentric, and express concerns about the wild animals that are my neighbors. An isolating mountain snow can have me stranded at home for a week. But I feel fortunate. When it all melts in the spring it nourishes fields of yellow wild-flowers that squish between my toes as I step out my front door. I watch meteor showers in the clear dark skies while lying in the truck bed of my old Chevy. I leave snacks for foxes to eat in the forest during harsh winter days. In other words, I am far away from the Philly girl I was growing up and used to be. Yet 212 classmates Kathryn Tessier and Lois Gatker made the trek to find me after our fortieth reunion.

Christmas morning we had a special treat. Valerie Elson posted the song "Christmas in My Soul" by Laura Nyro on Facebook for us to hear. She also filled in our memories of our lives in America fifty years ago when it was released. Many of us had turned the age of twenty, when we were our most idealistic for the truth on America's challenges of civil rights and profoundly the Vietnam War. Some of these deep divisions we are facing now as Baby Boomers, such as the racial reckoning in the protests of Black Lives Matter. And, the undeniable rise of fascism that has taken root under the Trump Administration cannot be overlooked; nor, the sobering rise of fake news and conspiracy theories. As I write we are not out of the woods, yet.

Fortunately, during a national crisis, we have Lois Gatker sharing her recipes and photos of her creative culinary skills on Facebook. So, the mood shifts a bit to something more positive than the realities of COVID and sedition. In essence, our growing relationships on Facebook over the years became an inexhaustible well of Divine Grace that imparts knowledge, renewal, and loving memories.

I was able to measure the depth of our wellspring of Divine Grace following the recent deaths of classmates Iris Chew and Brenda Cavalier. I was completely surprised by the sudden announcements posted on Facebook of their deaths, for they both continued to laugh at my jokes up to their very end. I also was often rewarded with their applause when I proclaimed I wanted to explore a new adventure. Neither one would allow me to feel despair for any reason even though they themselves were suffering. Yet from their Divine Grace I went on another day feeling renewed by their compassion.

Classmate Iris Chew loved the music of Laura Nyro so listening to "Christmas In My Soul" reminded me of the last time we spoke before she died. Iris had fooled me into thinking that we were going on a road trip together across the United States. I was expecting her arrival on my doorstep when I heard the shocking news that she passed away. Days earlier, she had left a message on my answering machine "to call her back." Iris never let on how sick she was when we talked long distance on the telephone. I had only seen her once in forty years after our reunion. But on the phone we allowed our fertile imaginations to soar, making a bucket list of places we were planning to go. New Orleans was high on our list because of the food and music; North Carolina's beaches beckoned. Iris had a paramour waiting in the wings she had not seen in a couple of years. Our voices were shrilled with mischief as we planned our adventure just like we were still teenagers sneaking out of Girls' High School to meet up with friends at Danny's restaurant.

In August 2020 I ended up driving across the country alone without Iris Chew. When I arrived at a destination on our bucket list, I talked to her in spirit, with memories of our younger days burning like an eternal flame. I maturely faced being left behind to face the challenges of the catastrophic hurricanes in the South and hundreds of wildfires burning relentlessly in the West that I had to navigate to make it home. I had to avoid people and eat at drive-thru restaurants during my entire journey because of COVID-19. I am still breathing.

Moreover, the recent news of the passing of Brenda Cavalier shocked me as well. For, until the moment of her death, she lifted me up from discouragement. Ironically, I didn't remember her socially from high school. I have not lived in Philadelphia for years. But I did remember her name from roll call as a kindred spirit. I loved her kind smile in her profile picture on Facebook which sustained me for years.

As I carry on, I have become accustomed to the sound of my own breathing and footsteps in isolation. COVID-19 has changed my existence entirely, but not all the changes have been bad. The Pandemic has made me closer to my family. For the first time we have engaged in monthly Zoom Chats.

Last night I stayed up late talking to my son by a wood fire. We shared a good bottle of bourbon, America's Native Spirit, as we discussed the state of the Union and our lives in flux. My son talked about moving abroad with his family which surprised me knowing how much he loves his home and friends. Although he lived and grew up abroad in Jamaica when he was a young boy. We moved to the West Indies in the 1970s to escape America's hideous segregation. At that time you could not find a picture of a black woman in a fashion magazine or billboard.

As my son continued to talk, our wood fire made me reflect on how homesick I used to get at Christmas time in the Caribbean. How I missed the cold, crisp, snowy days of Pennsylvania and the warmth of sharing our hearth with family and friends. I still have memories of the holiday ritual of Christmas lights and carolers singing near steam vents outside City Hall in downtown Philadelphia. And the gigantic organ that towered to the ceiling in Wanamaker's Department store would blare Christmas music with grandiosity while a light show streamed snowflakes in many colors. I hold these memories dear as my child faces the unknown of a different America. I keep quiet about my doubts. I had not seen my grandkids in months because of COVID-19.

I arose the next morning with a need to fix my country road. It became so rutted from winter rains that it became hard to drive for most people. I stopped receiving deliveries. It didn't bother me because my truck can make it up my driveway even when others could not navigate the holes. Before COVID, I was rarely home. Being single and retired I ate out most of the time hanging out in the "big city." I bathed at the swim club before heading to art classes. Times have changed. The COVID lockdown and resulting isolation has compelled me to finally fix my road. The more recent "surge" in COVID-19 has me spending my days quietly in the forest patching holes and listening to the birds singing. My social life has stopped like a broken time clock except from a social distance.

Fiddletown, CA
January 2021

Judy Chu Pembroke

A DAY IN A LIFE

IN THE EARLY HOURS OF THE MORNING, I SAT IN FRONT of my mother's vanity. The room was dimly lit. She picked up her brush and brushed out my night's knots in even, methodical strokes as she did each morning. But this morning would be different. This was the first day that I would step into the halls of a high school that my aunt had gone to some forty years before in the nineteen thirties. It was at a time before the war broke out in Europe and in most parts of the world. The school was called the Girls' Normal School, a school that was meant to groom the brightest and most talented girls from a very privileged society in Philadelphia. There were debutante balls and all the gilded trappings that went on among the elites. Later, the school had changed its name to the Philadelphia High School for Girls, and I would be the one to hold the family's tradition and mantle.

My mother was very proud of me. She had laid down my school dress, my undergarments, and even the grey sweater I would wear for the next four years. I had always wondered why the same grey simple sweater when other girls at the school wore such beautiful and colorful tops. All my mother would say was that grey matches everything.

My parents had just come out from the hellish nightmare of WWII in China. My father was a government official under the old regime, and the chief engineer of the southern railroad system for Chiang Kai-shek, the president of China. Because he had held a prestigious position, he fled from China with my mother when the Communists took over. In his teens, he attended Mercersburg Academy in Mercersburg, Pennsylvania, a preparatory school for boys, and then to the University of Pennsylvania and later Yale. As a young man in his twenties, he went back to China in the hopes to rebuild the nation after the fall of the Ching Dynasty and rise of the Republic. I was his little girl, his princess, and he had such great hopes that I would follow in his footsteps, a greatness that I have yet to achieve.

I was a puny child, small in stature, and had just reached puberty when other girls my age had blossomed into womanhood. I was also a very sickly child, with poor vision, and carried a birth defect in my heart. I was not pretty for sure, and certainly did not inherit my mother's beauty and grace.

As I stared into the mirror that morning, I had the whole weight of family tradition and my parent's expectations on me. I remembered that earlier that week, I had put away all my childish things - my dolls, my toys, and packed them away in their original boxes and stored them in the basement. I told my childhood friend of more than eight years that I could not play with her anymore. This was because I had to become more serious and to take my studies to heart.

Finally, after many do's and don'ts from my parents and a long and lonely train ride to the north side of the city, I arrived at the school. I joined a group of girls that had miraculously popped up from subway terminals from all over, dressed similarly like me, but without the grey sweater! We were ushered into the Grand Hallway of the school, where pink marble lined the walls, and a large grey marble statuette of Winged Victory of Samothrace or "The Goddess of Victory without a head" stood at the end of the corridor that led to the auditorium. The Goddess was created sometime before Christ to honor the Goddess Nike, and the battles fought in Macedonia at the time of the Romans. She represented a sense of action and triumph, a depiction of triumphant spirit and of the divine coming together. It was a good thing she did not have a head, so then I could become unnoticed, invisible, and hidden. I was not a great warrior, and in truth, I was a coward. I was scared to my bones. I could not fight this fight my parents wanted for me. I just wanted to blend in with the others and remain unnoticed.

The girls looked so bright and cheerful and I knew I would love them from the start. We made our way to homeroom and were assigned our seats according to our last name. I sat in the back, being that my last name was the last letter in my particular homeroom. Our schedules were given out for each class, and were marked by a time and period. Class officers were elected sometime that day. I was chosen to be the Treasurer and handle the bank accounts of the girls in my homeroom. It gave me a sense of fiduciary duty and the one position in which I could be comfortable. I was good with numbers and at the age of six I was taught arithmetic using the abacus.

Throughout the week, we got to know our teachers. The math and science teachers took to me and it was easy to absorb what they taught. It all came easily to me. They particularly liked my linear thinking, a skill that was critical in the sciences, a skill that was honed and encouraged by my father.

In the art department, I impressed no one. I drew leaves all through elementary and into junior high: leaves tilting right and leaves tilting left. But always the same leaf. It was not even a bunch of leaves from a single branch, but one singular leaf with no purpose or divine design. Small or big, it was the same leaf. My mind could not capture what I saw in nature and translate what I saw onto paper. One afternoon, I was in Miss Cohen's art class. I was drawing my leaf. She looked at it and then at me in utter dismay. Either she thought I had some hidden talent that was just about to emerge, or she thought I was just utterly stupid. I think she thought the latter, and she would have been right.

But where I found solace and contentment was in my English classes. There was Mrs. Rubinstein, my favorite. She opened a new world for me. She taught me to see the rawness of humanity, its despair, and its triumphs. She taught me the power of the word, how it could bring nations to its knees or it could depict the smallest fragility of the human heart. I wanted to absorb everything, to feel, to touch, to be alive in the most amazing way. How can one forget the passages in Hugo's Les Misérables showing the silhouette of Collette walking barefooted in the snow to fetch a bucket of water, and

Jean Valjean looking kindly and lovingly on her? Many years later, I read the book in French and that one passage tugged at my heart and soul, and it still does to this day. In Hugo's own words, the book details a progress from evil to good, from injustice to justice, from falsehood to truth, from hell to heaven, from nothingness to God. Can I learn from this great master? Can I write like him?

Now that I am older, I look back on those years with the warmest feelings of gratitude and love, especially for the friends I made there, for the teachers who nurtured me. No one can replace that. The Winged Victory shadows me wherever I go. She refuses to let me drift into mediocrity.

I had fulfilled my promise I made to my father. I held the mantle of my family's tradition and honor. In my fifties, I taught chemistry at Vanderbilt University. I presented a paper at the Joint Navy, Air Force, and Army Conference on Ballistic Predictions based on Thrust and Burn-Rate. I became known among military scientists, and formulated the propellant that is used today in our anti-missile missile systems in South Korea for the Defense Department.

However, my achievements pale in comparison to what I learned about the human heart - to be able to care and love those around us. More precious than gold, I need to understand their needs and their sufferings. I need to fill their souls with God's love. Our successes are fleeting, money can come and go, but love is what holds us together and endures forever. I will carry these ideals that I learned from the very halls of my high school throughout my life, and if God willing, I will carry it to my grave and beyond.

Je suis dans mon lit, un rêve réagisse,
D'un ange qui me suit, toujours mon complice,
Elle me chasse aux quatre coins du monde
Toujours parapluie moi par son ombre,
Je n'échappe pas à sa sagesse,
Même à la fin des temps ou de ma vieillesse.

Elle essuie mes larmes qui cours sur ma face,
Une tristesse qui reste toujours sur sa place.
Un poids qui loge dans mon cœur et mon âme
Je dois finir ce travail qui souvent m'alarme.
Elle est toujours là avec une aile étendue,
Elle ne me quitte jamais dans ma solitude.

Je suis dans les creux de mon lit,
Je caresse mon vieil ami,
Ma douleur s'enfuit et mon âme se réjouit
Dans le passage aux quatre vents je le suis.
Je ne suis jamais seul avec mon complice,
Je suis souvent mordue mais mon ange réagiss

Houston, TX
February 2021

Susan Dukow and Judy Bluebond-Seelig rekindled their friendship after forty years at the 212's 40th Class Reunion. Susan presented Judy a print she made of her while at GHS. It was one of five pieces of Susan's art that survived a 1970 flood in West Chester, PA.

Susan Dukow

1968. THE YEAR OF OUR HIGH SCHOOL GRADUATION,
the assassinations of Martin Luther King, Jr. and Robert F. Kennedy,
peaceful protests that turned violent in Chicago at the Democratic
National Convention, Apollo 8 and Hey Jude. We were young women
embarking into a world of wonderment after four years of an all-girls
scholastic preparatory school, a part of the Philadelphia Public School
system for the 'gifted.' The young women were from all over the city -
the Jewish girls, the Blacks, Asians, Irish and Ukrainians, and the Italian
'Subway Girls' from South Philadelphia. We believed this was normal.
We did not know then that our being together would forever reflect who
we would become. We were a group of innocents who were not allowed
to wear pants in school and it was the days before pantyhose. So yes,
there were garter belts to contend with and those awful gym uniforms –
sometimes with garter belt straps and stockings peeking out below on
the hockey field or the basketball court.

Quite a few, including myself, hated our days at The Philadelphia
High School for Girls; most loved it and fondly remember those years. In
our sophomore year we were traumatized when one of us died between
classes - a vivid memory for too many. The story goes from some who
were in class with her right before it happened, that a teacher had ridiculed her over her less than normal performance.

None of us really know how it happened to our classmate that day,
that she died. It was not spoken of at all except in our quiet traumatized
fifteen-sixteen-year-old whisperings. It was hushed and not further mentioned by counselors, teachers or even our parents. Today, likely a class
of teenagers would be counseled; in 1966 we were not, and we've come

to realize that we carried it with us all these years. So much speculation, beliefs and assumptions as to what transpired; and the profound heartbreak and perhaps even some guilt for her closest friends and her family. And as I write this, what about that teacher?

We were competitive and high achievers; at least some were; not me. I wound up in summer school every summer. I was busy cutting more classes than I attended, hanging out in Center City, going to movies, the art museum and being with older guys… and I paid for that; having nightmares for decades that I never actually graduated.

We were offered the opportunity to have a second diploma in either art or music. I opted for art and while all these years later, fifty plus, it took me that long to get over the insults and falsehoods of what was appropriate in making art, endured literally at the hands of the one wicked art teacher. I still recall her ripping a painting of mine off the wall one day during a class critique. Damn bitch traumatized me for fifty years.

It took me forty years to want to have anything to do with any of my classmates. Some memories, even of my closest friends, were not necessarily good ones - they didn't approve of my boyfriend of the time – and later, yes, they were correct not to. The feelings of 'less than' haunted me for decades. My move to California shortly after graduation had placed enough time and distance between me and the GHS experience, until one of my old pals tracked me down a number of years later. And years after that, she was beyond persistent that I should come to our fortieth reunion and it was then that I reconnected with so many of my other classmates in our 212 Class.

Leading up to the reunion there were phone calls with a few who had been my closest friends. Forty years with no contact is a long time… Judy Bluebond Seelig asked if I remembered her 16th birthday party and a fellow by the name of Paul who I apparently moved in on the night of her party. I was mortified when she reminded me of this, my recollection being quite vague and who wouldn't block that horrid behavior from their psyche? But dear Judy laughed it off and three hours later on our phone call it was as though no time - or my betrayal of her - had ever happened.

Dina Ghen reminded me of the cops coming to our art class looking for us because of a couple of things we'd thrown in our car on the way to school. They were meant to be art projects, but instead, became good old trouble.

Recently, Dina reminded me of a night at a party when I may have saved her from date rape. She said I'd been her protector – even when I was getting her into trouble. There were foggy recollections when she shared this with me – Dina in the back room with some boys - and my yelling at them, and at her, to get the hell away from those guys. With our hearts filled with the old love we had, we have now rekindled our friendship. A side note to all 212'ers: Dina has told me how she hated being 'Peter Pan', our class mascot, and resents how this ever happened to her; she wants names.

The memories kept poking at me; so many blocked and unable to recall. At the fortieth reunion, I met women from our class that I had no recollection of whatsoever, but several seemed to remember me; "one of the 'cool' art girls" they've said. What were they smoking? I was stunned to hear this having felt invisible during these years.

Five years later I flew back again for our forty-fifth reunion. However, by the time the fiftieth rolled around, I said to myself, enough, not going this time. My 212 classmates were still all so smart, educated and many remained quite opinionated, if not some needing to always have the last word on Facebook or group emails we shared between reunions. And my insecurities, or 'something' began to surface again - perhaps just uncomfortable, conflicted feelings.

However, as time has since passed, my feelings of 'less than' that had taken hold during my troubled adolescence eased. I finally began to feel more confident around my classmates as some gals came to visit me in Los Angeles and I found affection and appreciation for more than a few that I hadn't previously had, or for whom I never even knew. And too, discovered that I hadn't been alone in my uncertainties. What a load to have been lifted.

So now in 2020, as I write this, the COVID-19 Pandemic has consumed us. Somehow Donald Trump became President after our beloved Barack Obama. It was shocking – all of it. Our lives, as well as the rest of the globe were turned upside down. In early March of 2020 I went into my own self-imposed lockdown in Los Angeles, along with my four young cats and my art. Since there are no partners or kids, this meant a lot of time on my own as it has been most of my life, and since I had retired in 2012 from working thirty-six years in the motion picture industry. Having found my creative side again in 2018, I had my painting as an outlet, and I seemed to be making up for all those lost years, prolific beyond my wildest imaginations. But, like a lot of us, I found that I was incredibly hungry for human connection.

On our class's private Facebook page in May 2020 I posted, 'Anyone up for a Zoom visit?' With the 210 members on the private FB page (out of our class of 400+) about forty showed up to our first call. We began the journey of rediscovering old and now new friends. A lifetime of more than fifty years, with many of our classmates already gone. We were about to turn seventy years old - all of us - with lots of smarts, spirit and joy. At our fortieth reunion we had joked about going to Thailand for facelifts when we were turning seventy - special deals for multiples - and now we were seventy and we were not going anywhere.

Our Zoom visits have evolved over these months. First, we filled in one another with our lives since high school. Then politics entered the conversations. The killing of George Floyd, Ahmaud Arbery, and Breonna Taylor, and the countless other Black lives that had been taken. Quite a few of us found another level of understanding of how life was back in those pink marble halls of Girls' High when we shared just that - the halls and the teachers inside the classrooms. Our Black Sisters in the midst of the pandemic and the Black Lives Matter movement brought home to many of us this fact – while the white sisters were working on their high achievements, too, maybe experimenting with pot, being naughty, seeking out boys, hiding in plain sight and incognito, shy within their studies and experiencing, through no fault of our own, the 60's - our Black Sisters had a completely different reality that was only now being shared with us in this moment of unrest and simply, the insane world of 2020.

We have been a captive audience to each other. The visits have been both joyous, mind-opening and thought-provoking; and maybe for some, a feeling of regret for not knowing what others had experienced in and around this cocoon that was our school and our hidden lives at home. We were all so young, with very little life experience, but now we have begun to share our tears and the raw feelings that several of us had back then and are having now, in and around the pandemic - our age, losses, fears and loneliness, and as former Senator Barbara Boxer from California stated, 'Our Golden Years - now our Stolen Years'. No facelifts this year.

But we have each other. This reconnection is our incredible gift and why we have decided to share our individual stories in and around the journey that began at Broad Street and Olney Avenue in 1964 at the Philadelphia High School for Girls.

Sherman Oaks, CA
November 2020
www.SusanDukowArt.com

Kathryn Flynn Tessier

GHS MEMORIES AND OUR ENHANCED CONNECTIVITY DURING COVID

MANY WONDROUS GHS MEMORIES SWIRL THROUGH MY mind. It's been very difficult to select which ones to include for this story. Reconnections and enhanced communications with some of my old and new classmates during the pandemic have definitely heightened my recollections of those GHS days and have assisted greatly in my well-being today.

When I first entered those hallowed pink marble halls of GHS, I was thankfully accompanied by two of my closest and dearest old neighbourhood friends from junior high - Karen Israel and Judy Wong. They are still cherished friends.

We three amigos had developed very close bonds at Wagner Junior High. We survived and thrived in that very entertaining and eye-opening experience (cops in halls, etc). We had each other's backs already, so were perhaps not too overwhelmed by our next pubescent adventure, GHS.

Naturally, in high school, we followed different educational paths, as per our curricula. I had chosen to add a fifth major, art. I was in art classes daily for all four years. I met and cherished those many new artsy-fartsy friends, as we creatively spread our wings.

It is no surprise, then, that my two favourite GHS teachers were the best art teachers there: Ephraim Weinberg and Sheila Cohen. They were very engaging, creative, accessible, knowledgeable teachers. They encouraged us to expand our minds and excel in whatever we did.

In the academic realm, I was also blessed with some excellent math teachers and a superb physics teacher. I do not recall their names, but their passion for their fields and excellent teaching methods were contagious and enamoured me much to those arenas. I excelled in their classrooms. I don't really recall any of my English, history, or French teachers. They were nondescript. Although the French teachers must have been good, as my GHS French stood me in good stead when I moved to Quebec, Canada, in the late 1960s. More anon.

Another GHS teacher that had a lifelong impact on me was Dr. Faust. I was never in any of her English classes, but she hosted a club that opened my eyes to much more of the world news, views, and history than any other teacher. In those weekly, coed, Youth Interested meetings, I met many more like-minded folks and friends with a passion for helping to create a more compassionate and just world.

I am beholden to GHS for introducing me to the wonders of the visual arts and just, global socio-political realms. I have cherished, nurtured, and expanded those interests to this day. I majored in fine arts and international political economy (particularly human rights) in university. In addition, as my scientific curiosity was whetted and skillfully encouraged at GHS, I was thrilled with the opportunity to work with the highly esteemed CBC's (Canadian Broadcasting Corporation) TV science production unit, *The Nature of Things*, for over a decade, fulfilling my desire to be gainfully employed in a documentary film production arena. I also worked in national and local TV newsrooms.

Back to GHS: needless to say, I thoroughly enjoyed my years there. I met and made many friends, many of whom I've stayed in touch with over the years, with many thanks to social media and organizers of GHS reunions. I have very fond memories made at reunions (especially in Paris) and visiting classmates' homes over the years. I am thrilled that several of us have stayed in touch, regularly, electronically and by phone.

I cannot move on from that era without mentioning that I did not find that GHS was all hard work and no play during those critical years. The pressure to get great grades was indeed intense, but many of us knew how and where to party hearty! I cannot emphasize enough the life-long need to play, then and especially now. Then, many of us would hang out and chill at a fabulous local restaurant, Danny's, after and sometimes during school hours. In junior and senior years, some of us moved on to hang out more at downtown restaurants and folkie clubs.

My emphasis on re-learning how to play brings me to the significant nature of its essence, especially in these COVID times. I have found that the joyfulness and frequency of play has immeasurably increased my sense of well-being. Isolated as we are in our homes, I found that I had fewer playfulness options than before. Facebook Word games are fun, but not nearly as stimulating nor as engaging as our GHS Zoom chats.

Our very special re-connectivity with our sisters through social media, especially our Zoom chats, has been a godsend to me. We play, we laugh, we cry on them, even though many of us did not know one another way back when, in that very special era, in those times, in that place.

As our quarantined lifestyles have left many of us isolated from our normal pre-COVID lives, this renewed connectivity is an awesome balm. COVID fears and doubts have been wreaking havoc in our souls. Many are suffering horrendous losses. We are reaffirming and reinforcing our lives by sharing our stories.

Our GHS reconnection through social media has been a cherished blessing. I have largely remained a fly on the wall, for most of these Zoom chats because I have lived in Canada for more than fifty years. The COVID responses, lockdowns, death, tracking, and vaccination rates are not as severe as in the U.S. I would rather hear from others, both U.S. residents and other classmates who also live outside the U.S.

Yes, I did move from Philadelphia, more than fifty years ago, to Canada. My first husband and I decided to move here, to live in a more peaceful and just culture. We were extremely disenchanted with the local racist culture in Philly and the national war-mongering attitudes. We've never looked back.

I am honoured and blessed to have this golden opportunity to listen to and share many of our GHS memories and updates with my sisters, especially during these trying COVID times, on various social media formats.

It gives me such pleasure to be a part of this passionate and engaging community of women who give me such joy and strength these days. Naturally, we have each reimagined ourselves since our GHS days, in our many and varied ways. Notwithstanding our different cultures (and some dysfunctional childhoods, mine included) and paths taken, most of us have survived and lived to tell our exceptional stories. Thank you all.

Toronto, Canada
January 2021

Lois Gatker

SITTING ON A HILL AT THE CORNER OF BROAD STREET
and Olney Avenue in Philadelphia Pennsylvania is the Philadelphia
High School for Girls. It is an all-girls academic school and a part of
the Philadelphia public school system. Smart girls came from all over
the city to go there. There was no question that is where I would attend
high school.

Girls' High was no joke. I studied my ass off. I was convinced that
acceptance to a good college was the goal of my matriculation, and it
was of paramount importance. Had I not been accepted into Penn State's
main campus, I would have been mortified, and lost face. Having an
episode of severe depression, and inability to function, I was absent for
a month during my junior year at Girls' High.

Looking back at myself I looked much the same as many of my
classmates - a preppy teen, in my madras, Villager, and Liberty print
round collar shirts with the required initial pin, A-line skirt, ribboned
cardigan, high socks, and Weejuns. All of my clothes were purchased
from Brownies and Rubens, reject stores selling high-priced brands with
imperfections… seconds, with the labels snipped.

Guess I fit in; I really didn't care. I didn't participate in school activities, take class trips, or go to the prom. I had some friends at GHS, but
not many that I socialized with out of school. My hood girls and boys were
who I wanted to hang with. In seventh grade, I remember sleepovers with
Deena and Kim, and making a Lee Harvey Oswald voodoo doll from an
old puppet. It had a wooden head and a cloth body. We drew a heart on
the body with nail polish and stuck pins in it.

I used to go to Avis' house, hang out, and feel closer to the Beatles, when her mother would say, "aye Lois, got a fag?" We were allowed to smoke. Her parents' English accents delighted me, and Avis was cool with a dry humor I appreciated. Avis and I went to London, Florence, Capri and Positano in '78 after I graduated nursing school.

Paula G. became a friend at GHS. Her sweet sixteen, a great memory. Roberta C. drove Kim, Deana and me to Long Beach Island in her VW. I sometimes hung with Paula on South Street in the mid 70's when I returned from my first trip to California.

Spending the night at Josie and Marcy's gigantic apartment on Rittenhouse Square was an experience. I bought my Sgt. Pepper jacket at the Parlor around the corner from their place.

My yearbook had only a few signatures. My feelings about GHS is evident in some disparaging remarks I wrote next to classmates and teachers' photos sometime shortly after graduation. I also signed it myself from people I was not friends with. The funniest, from Kat, who I saw as a totally free-spirited beatnik hippie. "Dig your bag," I wrote," Luv, Kat." WTF. I'm sure Kat, who I now consider a friend, will get a kick out of that.

We graduated in '68 in our white dresses and went off to live our lives. By now the collegiate look was replaced by Carnaby Street and hippie garb. I shouldn't have wasted time fretting about being accepted to Penn State. I dropped out in about a month. I really didn't give a shit about rats in Skinner boxes. I hated dorm living. I wanted to be with my homies. Someone sold me some fake mescaline, and I was 'outta there!!'

In the interim, I've lived on both coasts. I was chased down Lookout Mountain in Laurel Canyon by residents with guns who didn't cotton to hippies, after the Manson murders. Soon after that incident, I hitchhiked while tripping on acid from L.A. to Santa Barbara in an Indian print bedspread, only to learn upon arriving that some boys had been found hacked to death in their sleeping bags on the beach! In the morning my thumb was out, headed back to The Hollywood Hills.

I hung out in ashrams, in the house of a Warlock with meth fueled bikers, a Harley in the dining room, and with wannabe made men from south Philly. I've had countless jobs: waitressed, been a maid, packaged dried flowers in a Dickensian basement in Germantown, taught crafts in a pre-school, worked on an assembly line, cooked in a health food restaurant, danced topless in New Jersey and Opa-locka, Florida, did cataloging for a philatelist, and worked as a RN in several hospitals in Philadelphia and the surrounding areas.

In June of '73, I was persuaded to move to Lawrence, Kansas with a friend who was a Playboy bunny. She had been living with a sociopath who was given a new identity and transplanted to Kansas for being a rat. In Soprano terminology, that's a tattletale of the worst kind. He hit her, the Feds moved him to California, and I moved to Kansas. Picking up her car that made it to Chicago caused me to be in the Federal building's parking garage where I was given the opportunity to spit on the designated space assigned to Judge Julius Hoffman. I never forgave him for the trial of the Chicago 7 and what he did to Bobby Seale. Unfortunately, my friend forgave the rat soon after we arrived in Kansas, and I accompanied her to Sacramento, where he was placed.

Learning of my father's death, which my mother was unable to communicate to me when it happened, and unable to tolerate my situation, I left them in Sacramento and moved to Redondo Beach, California. I stayed with a Philly friend until I found an apartment and got a job cocktail waitressing on the pier. On a trip with Larry, a friend from Philly, to Ensenada, Mexico, looking for brass beds to buy and sell, something happened. I was ejected from the convertible VW, (the top was NOT down; divine intervention?), crushing three vertebrae, cracking several ribs and other injuries. I have amnesia. The first day I remember is Christmas, fifteen days later. I asked a friend why everyone from L.A. came to visit except Larry. I was told he was killed instantly.

The American consulate had notified my friends who arranged an ambulance to take me to the hospital of the University of San Diego.

I'm told when I saw palm trees out the window when we arrived, I said, "Oooooo, are we in Miami?" The consulate also called my mother and told her to come and to be prepared to possibly make arrangements to transport my body. My body was alive when my mother arrived, and the doctors told her I may not walk again. I did, eventually. I stayed in the hospital for one month. The great nursing care I received is why I am a nurse today.

My last nursing positions were at the Crisis Stabilization Unit and the Addictions Receiving Unit in the county where I live on the Gulf coast of Florida. It is a challenge treating someone with a swastika tattoo who is high on methamphetamine, has hooks implanted in his chin that can rip you open with one head butt, and is smashing his fists on the window that separates you while cursing you out. Entering that room to bandage his hand, I was grateful for the large man who accompanied me to provide protection.

Pulling down someone who hung themselves in the shower is not something you forget quickly. My nursing career has been trying at times. I even went to Beauty School and got my Esthetician license in 2007 because I was fed up with nursing administration. I have not forgotten the packet of letters I have from patients and their families, thanking me for the care I gave. All in all, my nursing career has been very rewarding.

Fast-forward to our 40th reunion. I came to the end of an event down by the river after the luncheon and then afterward to a party at Audrey's, Candy's sister. It must have been the next day, I had a crew of classmates come to my house up in the country for dinner and conversation. It was a blast.

Another reunion time, Avis drove the two of us to a get-together on Long Beach Island that Anita hosted. I had a conversation with Ellen. I don't think I ever spoke a word to her while at school. Same with Anita. What great women... all of them.

The following year my life became a sad country western song.

My home was flooded, I broke my leg, my job ended, my pets died or ran away after the flood, so it was time for a change. I had connected with classmates via Facebook. Anaiis (Wendy) came up to the country and provided some computer education. We weren't friends in school. From high school days, I had a photo of her at Halloween, dressed as a wraith, sunken black hollows for eyes, a white ghostly face, wrapped in a bloody American flag; her protest to the Vietnam war. I wore a sheet gathered about my neck with 5 cents marked on the front; I was a nickel bag. Our costumes speak volumes about where our heads were at the time.

Connecting with an old Jr. high friend after the flood, I learned she was looking for a roommate. I flew out to investigate L.A. She lived in Studio City, not far from Susan, who picked me up, and took me to her house. She took me out to eat to a great place, and she left me with a stash. Another one I don't think I ever said a word to at school.

From L.A. I flew to Sacramento where Rachel came for me, and took me to her home. All I knew about Rachel, from at school, was that she was wild, associated with the totally arty hippies, like Kat and Psylvia, and that she ran away to California with her boyfriend. This stranger was coming to get me at the airport with an open heart and home. On her days free, she took me to her house up north, to the Yuba river and to San Francisco. She took me to dinner at the Slanted Door. If anyone knows San Francisco, this is a major restaurant. We went for foot massages, too.

From Rachel's, Paula came and got me and took me to her spread. Stargazer Ranch is beautiful, and I never saw the sky like I did there. We went to wineries for tastings and she took me to her athletic club. After a long visit, she schlepped me to the airport to fly back to Bucks County.

These women were the net that caught me after my world fell apart. They didn't have to be there for me, but they were, and I am eternally grateful.

While in California, I spoke to an old friend, explaining to her that I was looking for a warm place to settle. She was down on the Gulf. I eventually made it here just before the new year of 2012. I bought my first house two and a half years ago.

With a pandemic and lockdowns in place, I feel like I acquired a bunch of new friends as these 212 connections continue to flourish. I have enjoyed our Zoom conversations. I am in awe of many of my classmates' accomplishments, liking more of them as time goes by, and am delighted at what totally cool women we've all become.

Gulf Coast, FL
December 2020

Dina Ghen

COVID-19 GAVE A NEW MEANING TO BEING ALONE... alone is alone is alone.

The idea of being alone is not new to a lot of us. We are used to solitude - some without husbands or children to begin with, or having been widowed or divorced by this time in our lives. But having a few friends and special interests are what keeps us going.

For me, I've been on my own since 1999 when my husband Max died. But I threw myself into my work as a massage therapist, reflexologist, teacher and yoga instructor. I had cats I'd rescued when I was in NYC, but I don't have any now; I didn't want to go through everyone dying at once again. Most of my clients at the time had died from cancer and AIDS and then my husband, and my elderly cats all left me alone in about a year and a half 's time.

Being alone after that never bothered me that much because I traveled for yoga, and I made sure these trips included seeing my niece and nephew. So, throughout the years it broke up some of the isolation, plus it was fun.

During an intensive practice with my yoga teacher not long ago and before the pandemic hit, during one of his regular early morning pontifications, he asked us what we would do without any 'have-to's' in our lives or needs to meet a schedule. It was like a prophecy. Who would have ever thought it would happen?

My life has taken a different turn. I have no teaching preparation to do for my yoga students and no yoga teacher to walk to. Not being able to travel to see family or to do yoga workshops, a planned trip to Scotland and beyond… like to Outer Hebrides when that fell through, has given me pause. Why should my seventieth birthday have been any different than my others that never materialized? Chuckle. Chuckle. COVID-19, that's why.

In the beginning of the lockdown, I was talking to Susan Dukow, one of my Girls' High classmates and friend from back then. I call her "Boss Susan" because she lovingly pushed me around fifty years ago, and now was doing it again, making me write this piece... well, we both agreed we liked being alone in this pandemic lockdown thing. The restrictions made it a little more extreme but who ever thought it would last this long? Now it feels more challenging.

Simply put, my day is pretty full with Zoom: Yoga, Pilates, Jewish Studies, Boss-Susan Zoom... I cook more now for myself, along with my shortened yoga practice and long walks through Center City Philadelphia. And occasionally I drop in on Girls' High Zoom, but mostly not. It's a good thing Susan is doing. A very good thing and I love her for it.

One of my best pleasures was discovering that Susan was painting again and that her paintings are a delight. And getting back in touch with my old art buddy on that level and talking about the process of creating and painting and creative thoughts and conversations stimulates me once again... with my old friend.

Her kitty videos make me laugh and give me much joy. Rediscovering that friendship has been a big boon for me.

My Jewish studies - Tea for Torah, well there happens to be GHS graduates in class. I'm 212, Julia 213 and Audrey 214! What a shock that was to discover off-handedly one day. I really do love the Jewish studies with the Rabbi and his wife. One small gap that is filled once or twice a week when I am with them and to feel a part of something worthwhile.

Of course, I've been watching CNN, PBS and MSNBC during this time. Needing to keep apprised of what was going on in politics took up its fair share of my time. In the election I did my part for the Biden Campaign, knocking on doors and working the phones.

Here in Philadelphia we had a lot of protests and some violence over the escalation of killings of innocent Black men and women.

Everything upside down, inside out and the world and our country in shambles. However, I do believe we will come out better, that there is hope with the Biden administration - when we get rid of the monster.

What's interesting about this time as we are older, all the other years up to this moment, most of us had the freedom to do what we wanted, go where we wanted. And now, most of us are in our senior years and we need to think how we are going to move forward, safely. With this virus too, many are not following protocol – not wearing masks, distancing, etc. How will we handle another virus – when it comes?

Within the last week I've had some terrible news, a yoga friend has been stricken with a fast-moving cancer and is in hospice. Our yoga community notified us for each to send him a video of our love and support. I did a selfie video to send to him and it was really difficult on many levels - just like writing this story is - but I got it done with a little help from my other Tinker Bells in high tech! Richard, my friend received it right on the appointed schedule and it gave him much joy. I suppose we all are reinventing ourselves on a daily basis because we must… because of COVID. But there are blessings in it all.

There have been births in my family and deaths that are more natural, but friends and family can't congregate to celebrate or grieve. That part hurts.

The lockdown that was supposed to be two weeks turned into lockdown for months, violence and rabid politics.

If asked about my time in COVID months ago, I would have said, 'no problem,' but now - alone is alone is alone. COVID deaths, the truth about Trump, his resistance to accept his loss and aid in the transition… it feels like it will never end. But it will.

Biden wins but Trump's Washington has thrown us under the bus and so it continues – for now.

What makes all of this very hard for me right now is that a friend and colleague is quickly dying of cancer. And I can't be there, hold his hand, make him laugh, but I did make a video to send to him. A little piece of me I could give to him.

Here is my paper, this is it. COVID is not over and unfortunately, we have other viruses that will come in the future, and we are still not prepared. Things will never be the way they were, just as after 9/11. And this change is a tremendous change because technology has played such a major role in communication. Where would anyone of us be without Zoom right now? How people will work, go to school and see their doctors is forever different. The virtual world is and will become more and more dominant.

We don't even know much now about these vaccines except their efficacy; and we won't know for years the good and bad of them – only that we had to get moving on them and do it as fast as we are. How will we cope with the next one? I know many don't want to think about it... but we must ask what have we learned from this isolation, loss of life and horrendous threats to our democracy with over half the population not accepting the election results and being okay with the way things have been handled. Our democracy is at risk. The toxicity of four years of Trump, culminating in his lack of response to COVID-19 leaves us in very uncertain times.

Is this all a reflection of where the world is today? We must ask ourselves these questions quickly and do something about it even faster. Ask too, with our Democracy being questioned and nearly destroyed, with Climate Change and COVID – will these things be our Flood?

Philadelphia, PA
December 2020

Psylvia Gurk Tessler went to Woodstock in 1969. Early one morning, she told us that while musicians jammed, she danced and photos were taken. Later, this one appeared in Life Magazine. The photograph has become iconic whenever Woodstock or hippies are mentioned. Psylvia said, "she never understood exactly why these images are so popular and hoped it's because people see something of joy and self-expression that speaks to them."

Psylvia Gurk Tessler

COVID DIARY

WEDNESDAY, DECEMBER 2, 2020

I just spent most of an hour looking for my granddaughter's college address. Then I called her mother for it and found her letter as soon as I had put the address into my phone.

I miss my brain.

I am constantly bargaining with myself. How about I get my mask and gloves and go to the post office and mail my granddaughter the carefully wrapped and boxed persimmons we picked yesterday at my daughter's house. Not her mother. In fact, of my three daughters and two granddaughters, only one of them is related to me by blood. Not telling which one.

And while I'm out, how about I stop off at the variety store to get some stickers to send to my grandnephews and the pet store for treats for my granddogs?

What am I thinking? I can't go to places unless absolutely necessary.

At least we live in a small town on a hill, so I can take a walk seeing hardly anyone. Good enough for now.

THURSDAY, DECEMBER 3, 2020

Today I was going to go to the farmers' market, but we have enough food to last until Sunday's market.

FRIDAY, DECEMBER 4, 2020

Already I am neglecting my journal. All is forgiven, though.

SUNDAY, DECEMBER 6, 2020

Slipping along - slow minutes, fast weeks. Wearing a bra and real clothes almost every day to take a walk or go to an appointment that must be in person. Finding Zoom very tiring. After one, I want to lie down and play games or read on the iPad.

WEDNESDAY, DECEMBER 9, 2020

The days do zip past, when they're over; each day dwindles slowly while it's happening.

TUESDAY, DECEMBER 15, 2020

Postcards to voters in Georgia are finished. I have to hope this runoff election will result in Democratic control of the senate.

I had to force myself to take my walk today, as usual. It's beautiful outside. The TV and computer games will still be here when you come back. Always bargaining.

Can't can't can't can't. Well, maybe.

I'm feeling affected by last Sunday's Zoom call with my high school class.

I went to an all-girl, academic track, all-city high school in Philadelphia that we all call Girls' High.

The women who I see on Zoom are real in every way. Being who they are, and being responsible and beautiful and smart and creative.

I didn't go to the fortieth, forty-fifth or fiftieth reunions. Wish I'd been there, but I couldn't justify the expense, spending all our money on a short trip like that.

The Zooms are a lot like the reunions, except that you can't really have separate conversations. Those are blooming, though, and emails and phone calls are beginning and are welcomed.

WEDNESDAY, DECEMBER 16, 2020

I can't believe that my nails are so long already, and my pillboxes have only three days left. Including today! I'm taking this personally.

What about saying "Each and every"? Aren't they interchangeable? Whenever I hear someone use that expression, I lose everything they say after that, trying in my mind to use only one or the other to see if it changes the meaning.

I realized I wished I had thought of keeping a shelter-in-place Covid19 journal. Then my high school classmates suggested we do it together as a project, each one adding her experiences to the rest. I wanted to write my own, not influenced by what others were saying.

I started. I didn't want to read the rest. I didn't want to read them. Then I read them.

Whoa! My women are such an awesome group of creative survivors, smart and beautiful and genuine.

I trust them. I admire them, every one.

Now I'm stuck. The last three nights, I have woken at 4:30 AM, and immediately am filled with memories, wishes, love and hope for my classmates. I don't have a choice; I need to write more. It needs to be more Girls' High oriented. Okay, for now. Can you tell I have fear of commitment? Back in the before time, I never wanted to take a plate at a party. Just carry a bit of food around eating it.

Not going to Girls' High was never a choice for me. In our family, you went to GHS or Central, and then to college, although my father didn't finish high school and neither of my parents went to college.

As a child, the library was my haven, and I asked the librarians if one could go to college to be a librarian. Because if not, well, that wasn't going to be a choice for me.

I don't remember my early impressions of the school, only that I hated the hypocrisy of the administration, and was puzzled by the snootiness of many of my fellow students.

I made friends, was thrilled to be going to school with my third cousin, Beverly, and tried to carry my books in a way that didn't injure me.

I shared a locker with Octavia. She was so tolerant of my being organizationally impaired, always had a bright smile and she was a high spot in my day. She told me the name her family called her. I understand about people sometimes having a true name that they don't reveal casually, and it was with respect and gratitude that I received the gift of hers.

Over the course of my student life, I cannot count the number of times different groups of us heard the phrase, "There are Girls' High girls, and there are girls who go to Girls' High."

I fell into the latter category. Perhaps I dove in face first.

Also, Dr. Thompson showed us how to sit down in front of the mirror to make sure our skirts didn't ride up too high. Perhaps a foreshadowing of Sharon Stone in *Basic Instinct*?

"Most of the girls at Girls' High are well-behaved. There are a few who spoil it for the others." Heard that often. We became "The Spoilers," an open group who met outside on the grass above the corner of Broad and Olney. We thought we were so bad, throwing down a quarter to the soft pretzel guy on the corner who would throw us back five pretzels, spread with mustard. We thought we were so bad, running away at lunch to drink sodas at the luncheonette and running back so as not to get caught. We thought we were so bad, hanging at Rittenhouse Square. I was one of the few who didn't smoke, so when a teacher came around the corner and everyone ran, I stayed put and refused to name names.

Remember when we refused to participate in air raid drills? They put us dissidents deep in the office, farther away from windows and outside walls and pissed us off even more.

I loved my friends at Girls' High. No, no list. Lists always leave somebody out. What should I do? I made a partial list that calls to me. Delete me; don't delete me. People have feelings whether we want to or not. Suffice it to say there were people at that school who made my life worth living.

I didn't get to hang out after school because I always had an after-school job. When did I do my homework, you ask?

Generally, I didn't.

I liked learning, and I liked expanding my horizons racially and culturally. I didn't like being chastised for failing to strive for standards that were old, outdated and arbitrary.

Hope I can fall asleep and stay asleep tonight. Good night. Sweet dreams.

THURSDAY, DECEMBER 17. 2020

Took a walk, did all my physical therapy exercises. Still haven't cut my nails. Made a bean stew in the oven. Supposed to be cassoulet. Except it's a hippie form of cassoulet.

Everything I make is a hippie version. Can't do it any other way.

It rained last night and so I need to scatter some seeds in the backyard.

I live in a small town, a little north of San Francisco. I love it here. There are things I miss about San Francisco, where I lived most of my adult life. A lot of those things aren't there anymore. I am happy here. Didn't feature myself for small town life, but it's good for an old woman who is shrinking and becoming more and more invisible. It's full of nature and beauty here, and that fills me with joy.

FRIDAY, DECEMBER 18, 2020

I believe that there are people who get dressed in real clothes with real underwear every day. I believe there are people who have so many pairs of loose, stretchy pants that they change into new ones every day. I believe there are people who don't turn on their televisions until the evening, or not at all. I believe there are people who shower daily, pick up books and read them with comprehension, organize the piles of papers into an order that makes sense.

I have been most of those people in my past lives, and I know some of them, but I am not one of them now.

I moved to San Francisco to visit Rachel, and lived in her house with her and her family in their commune for about six months. I was and am grateful to Rachel for her hospitality and for getting me to the place that immediately felt like home.

MONDAY, DECEMBER 21, 2020

Half my exercises are done. Loving the cold weather, but only two days of rain so far this month. That's not good news. Hoping for no drought.

Finished my daily Portuguese lesson on duolingo.com. Studying a language that I can use with my Brazilian daughter whom I adopted as an adult. She is happy that I'm learning her language; she's completely fluent in mine.

Happy Solstice!

SUNDAY, DECEMBER 27TH, 2020

Just got back from the farmers' market. Enjoying my morning lemon water with … LISBON LEMONS! My favorite. And, yes, they do deserve all that yelling.

Not many farmers there; only about half the usual booths. They deserve a week off from their grueling, physically and emotionally demanding work schedules. I wouldn't want to have to deal with these entitled people.

MONDAY, DECEMBER 28, 2020

How are people so excited for a new year, like it will end racism and COVID?

WEDNESDAY, DECEMBER 30, 2020

So many people I know are single, which means they are alone. Some of them get groceries delivered, so they don't even see people at the market.

I have a partner, and we are very compatible, and it's more than lucky for both of us. Our bubble is the two of us, two of our daughters. The father of my daughter, and her housemate are also in our bubble by default. Our bubbles are the same.

THURSDAY, DECEMBER 31, 2020

Last day of 2020. Not much change expected, except on letters and checks, neither of which we use much anymore.

SATURDAY, JANUARY 2, 2021

Happy New Year!

THURSDAY, JANUARY 7, 2021

Yesterday, the orange guy ranted and raged and fomented an insurrection. Redcaps with white skin broke down barriers, broke into the capitol in D.C., damaged the building and delayed the counting of the electoral ballots. Late at night there, the counting went on. The dicknose lost.

I was busy doing things all morning and didn't have any media input until about 1PM. I saw young white men inside and outside the building, and several kinds of law enforcement treating them gently. Nothing like the gassing when the protesters were protesters and peaceful.

Then I heard that a woman was shot. Still don't know anything about that. I drank my smoothie and went to the post office to mail my sister a birthday package. I was so upset that I mentioned it to the post office employee who helped me. She told me not to turn on the television any more.

This is part of why I wanted to keep a COVID diary.

THURSDAY, JANUARY 21, 2021

Yesterday, Kamala Harris and Joe Biden were inaugurated! I am hopeful and a great weight is lifting off of my spirit.

Already, positive changes are being made. The Muslim ban is lifted. The country is rejoining the Paris agreement and the Keystone pipeline has been stopped. More vaccines have been ordered, deportations stopped.

This old normal cheers me and I'm ready to hear more positive news.

MONDAY, JANUARY 25, 2021

Feels as though it's been a while. My partner has an appointment on Friday for the vaccine. Because they're giving them to people over seventy-five now.

Had two daughters here for three nights. They were going to sleep over, then another and another. I was thrilled, and had a lot of fun with my bubble. After they left, though, I was very tired.

I have some delicious flannel pajamas that I was keeping to give for a present if someone came over and needed something warm and cozy. Hah! I kept them for myself and I wish I had done that a long time ago. Nothing like a shower and those pajamas on a cold, rainy day. They're pink with black polka dots.

FRIDAY, JANUARY 29, 2021

The feeling of being a little more relaxed is lasting. I'll believe it when I see it, though. The personal is, as it always has been, political. Black lives matter. "No justice, no peace" has replaced, "What do we want? (_____); when do we want it? Now!"; and the ever popular, "El pueblo unido jamás será vencido," which can be translated as,"The women, united, will always be delighted." Joking, joking. I have chanted that latter one as well, though.

But, really, what do I know? I haven't marched in protest in two years, and then it was just here in my little town.

TUESDAY, FEBRUARY 2, 2021

Then I woke up, and it was all a dream…

No self-respecting author would say that. Certainly no one who went to Girls' High. It worked in Alice's Adventures in Wonderland, and never again since.

Fairfax, CA
December 2020-February 2021

Susan Halpern Rosenfeld

SO, WHO MAKES NEW
FRIENDS AT SEVENTY???

REWIND TO THE SPRING OF 2020. THIS NOVEL CORONA-
virus is beginning to pervade our daily existence. What was once
normal and routine is now gone from our calendars. Activities and
meetings are cancelled. The ever-popular doctor appointments and
procedures are now being postponed and rescheduled, soon to be
further rescheduled. Life has changed!!!!!

CNN became my daily go-to TV channel, replacing mindless HGTV
episodes of House Hunters. The reporters and commentators were my
source of information. My level of interest about this pandemic could be compared to watching a train wreck. You don't want to look, but you cannot pull
yourself away. I became increasingly more involved in the 2020 Presidential
election. My husband and I could often be heard ranting and cursing about
the drama and the craziness that accompanied the political arena.

Twice-daily neighborhood walks with Jerry, known as our Senior
Strolls, allowed us to exercise, relax, and speak, albeit socially distanced,
with others we met along our route. I actually walked so much that my newly
diagnosed arthritic knees are now being rehabilitated in physical therapy
sessions. Apparently, I pushed myself beyond my limits to achieve the
coveted minimum of ten thousand daily steps, as measured by my FITBIT.

Cooking became a more frequent activity in the Rosenfeld house-
hold. Suddenly, planning meals and shopping for groceries to be delivered
or picked up curbside became the new way. I felt like a new bride again,
waking up thinking of the meals planned for the day. My dishwasher was

probably in shock being run three times a week instead of its previous maybe three times a month usage. Credit card expenditures were basically from three places... the supermarket, the pharmacy and, of course, Amazon. This trifecta has continued to this present day. Who could have ever predicted that this stay-at-home behavior would continue for so long!

However, all is not gloomy. Family drive-by visits are precious. We now appreciate purchasing that package of BOUNTY or CHARMIN, despite being limited to just one of each. Having a tank of gasoline last for several weeks is a plus. New clothing makes no sense because no one sees you anyway, and you can safely repeat outfits for days on end.

Suddenly, new words were in our vocabulary: Covid-19... pandemic... hybrid-education... PPE... and closest to my heart, ZOOM, having its own group of words such as Mute and Unmute. Perhaps, the initiation of our 212 Zoom meetings, introduced to us by our own Susan Dukow, has been so pivotal to new beginnings. Contained in those little squares on our screen are friends, both old and new. What a wonderful opportunity to have conversations with girls we may have known, back in the day, but more importantly to have the chance to meet women we may not have crossed paths with during our days in school.

We have become a small, but mighty group of religiously diverse, ethnically different, and geographically varied sisters. Some are quite verbal. Others, like myself, sit quietly, but are involved in listening to the high level of involvement and civic responsibility that my classmates possess. We came to Girls' High from a variety of neighborhoods. We experienced meeting others from areas that I had previously only just heard about: The Subway Girls from South Philly, the girls from West Philly, those from Logan, North Philly, and the Northeast. We meshed and created a welcomed change from what was, for me, a more segregated K-8 experience growing up in Mt. Airy.

So, in answer to the question I posed at the beginning... Who makes friends at age seventy?? **THAT WOULD BE ME!**

Lafayette Hill, PA
December 2020

Sandra Heginbothom Lewis

LIFE DURING THIS COVID PANDEMIC HAS NOT BEEN SO different from my life before it, except that I was furloughed from my part-time 'gig' at Luzerne County Community College where I still teach and tutor under a grant from Goldman Sachs. I have missed the theatre trips to NYC and Canada which my partner, Bob, and I have taken for the last five years, but they will happen, again, in 2021 or 2022. I have been bored, but have done more pleasure reading, needlepoint and gardening. My garden was the best it has ever been this past summer because I had the time to spend up to ten hours a week trying to tame it into shape. I have not yet gone back to doing watercolor or photography, as I used to do.

Socializing with other people from the Susquehanna University 'family' was done sparingly in backyards and porches and stopped as the infection rate in our community finally caught up with the rest of the state and country. But socializing with me always seems to happen with a husband's or partner's group of friends. Not ones that I have cultivated... I would be hard pressed to think of calling someone to go out to lunch or to a movie.

So, I'm used to being a loner. Probably always have been based on the way I was raised. Except for my youth group at Elkins Park Episcopal Church, I never really did many activities outside my family 'pod'. I've had loads of 'friends' but only in a very superficial way.

I was an only child who lived with my mom, dad and Nana. We did everything as a unit. My mother was a 'stay-at-home' mom who walked me to school early on, worked with the PTA and helped with homework. She so wanted me to play school or paper dolls when I wanted to do activities with my dad and Nana. They taught me how to cook, sew, garden and do repairs around the house. She did teach me to paint, and enrolled me in ballet classes which met on Saturdays in Germantown (Miss Jean's). There were no afterschool activities, however. That was homework time or joint TV watching. We went to church on Sundays and then, out to eat.

Vacations were done the same way in the summer, as a unit; either a two-week car trip up and down the east coast, or into Canada or time in Cape May, NJ at the Seacrest Inn. I had cousins on my father's side who were my age and second cousins on my mother's side. But other than an occasional birthday party or picnic dinner, I did not see them much. There is a reason for this… my mother had TB while in high school and spent quite a chunk of time in Temple Hospital and was always afraid of my getting sick or getting polio. She was told not to try to have children, but her mom and my dad and she decided to take the risk. So, I was that gift they were not expected to have and did not want to lose.

Things changed when I was ten and I spent my first summer at Lighthouse Art and Music Camp with Beth, Carla, and Wendy and then, at a NSF science program at Hahnemann Hospital. The only weird thing is, other than Wendy, all my "friends" were Jewish, and even though I learned a lot about their culture, celebrations, and love of music and education, I was a tangential member of their group. I went to GHS, and then Mount Holyoke College, both female and both demanding. I was in school to educate myself... not to socialize and party.

So, as I said, living during this time period has not been that stressful and the use of FB and these Zoom meetings with my classmates from GHS have been entertaining, especially reading the posts from many of you. I, also, have the problem on FB of keeping my group of Uncommon Women from HS separate from those from MHC; so many interesting and independent women who all ended up politically the same. We've all done well in our different ways and should be proud of ourselves no matter how we were when we were younger.

Selinsgrove, PA
February 2021

Karen Israel

I'M STILL STANDING

I GREW UP IN BEAUTIFUL EAST OAK LANE. THE HOUSES were big and the streets tree-lined. Thanks to my mother's incredible green thumb, our property was endowed with rose bushes, forsythias, azaleas, dogwood trees, hydrangeas and many other flowers, too. For me our backyard was always a place of happiness, fun, and serenity; and it was always filled with kids. Even from a young age, I remember the neighborhood kids were always at our house, whether it was softball, touch football, tag, hide and seek, badminton, croquet, or just a picnic. Our house was the place to be. This was in part because my parents had an open-door policy. It did not matter who you were or where you came from.

Until the Pennsylvania College of Optometry built dormitories, we rented our third-floor to two of the students. Although I must have been around three years old, I remember that so many other future eye doctors congregated in our house to cram for finals. There was the sweet, wonderful smell of my mother's homemade apple pies and pots of brewing coffee. Life was good.

Before I entered Girls' High I always liked school. I studied, did my homework and projects. I liked most of my teachers and schoolmates. Junior High was the best. That's where I met my lifelong sisters, Kat Flynn Tessier and Judy Wong Greco. We were the Three Musketeers.

I hated every second, minute, hour and day at GHS. From day one, I suddenly felt insecure, tense, nervous, fat, ugly and stupid. All I saw were beautiful, studious girls who seemed to know each other. I couldn't find any of my friends. I felt alone. Of course, I did make lovely friends over the years, one of which was Sherrie Harabin. She became my friend on the first day of school. She saw me standing alone in the lunchroom, walked over, and tapped me on my shoulder. We were both new freshmen, and neither of us knew anyone. We bonded immediately. Although we never shared any classes, we were in study hall together. We both had parents who would not let us have long hair. She would sit behind me, and I would hang my head over the back of the chair. She would then make a mark to see how much my hair had grown. The next time I would do the same for her. She was a brilliant student and a kind and compassionate human being. Sadly, one day in March of 1966, she tragically passed away. It was my first experience with death. I was so devastated by her loss that I was unable to attend school for a week afterward. It was one of the most traumatic experiences of my life.

I couldn't grasp algebra or geometry, despite having private tutors for both subjects. In 11th grade I was bullied and berated by a certain algebra teacher who would read my test scores out loud to the entire class. I had migraines almost every day. Well, I made it through the class despite his constant ridiculing, but I did have to attend summer school for a better grade.

In addition to my struggles with math, I also had to deal with comments about my looks. I would overhear being called fat and fat-assed. There were also remarks about my hair. Although it was not all of the time; once is quite enough to indelibly lodge in your brain.

I liked a few teachers. Those were the classes in which I received decent grades. My only favorite class was 11th grade American history with Mr. LaPaglia. He was tall, thick and goofy-looking, but I adored him. His teaching technique was casually sitting in front of the class on a stool. Many of us took advantage of him and ate in class, sneaking gum, chips and snacks. He finally, after many reprimands, made a secret pact with us, that if noshing during class helped us focus, he'd allow it. Unfortunately, two days later, it came to an end. Somebody blabbed and ratted him out. I was thoroughly ticked off. His exams were in essay form. YAY! I wrote my answers in pen. How did he know I had a burning desire to be a journalist? I got all A's. I loved the fact that he was always nice to me. He would give me his clean coffee cup, have me fill it with cold fountain water, and put in my celery and carrot sticks so that they could stay cold and crispy. I was in teenage love.

Anyway, since I was the ultimate Beatlemaniac, my inside locker was adorned with photos of "My Boys". That drew lots of attention. When Beatle tickets for Convention Hall went on sale, I couldn't go to the city to get them. Too obvious. So, I coerced my girl, Judy Wong, to pretend she was sick and get them! Of course, she did, and returned home eight hours later. I had to tell her mom so that she didn't worry. This is why I still love my Judy.

I loved our 50th reunion. I found out things I never knew, such as I wasn't the only girl who went to summer school, hated some teachers, felt sad, struggled, etc. It was so cathartic for me. But I loved renewing friendships. I am so thankful to have been a part of this wonderful experience.

As an avid animal lover, I have been blessed to have spent part of my life with two beloved dogs. Cody, a handsome male Labrador mix, was my first. After he passed away, I adopted Logan, a beautiful female shepherd mix. Although both have crossed the Rainbow Bridge, each one has left a precious paw print on my heart.

I may not have attended college, but I had a wonderful career as a corporate travel agent for thirty-plus years. Although, now, I may be legally blind, I'm still standing! Singing it loud!

Glenside, PA
February 2021

Terry Jones Candis' coffee table serves food for the soul.

Terry Jones Candis

IDENTITY AND
JUXTAPOSITION

ACROSS THE SPAN OF SIX PLUS DECADES, I'VE endeavored to consider who I am in the context of my environment. What were the building blocks that helped define my identity? I conclude that from my beginning, juxtaposition, right place at the right time, was paramount. Home was a row house in North Philadelphia. Mom and Dad were the busy adults and I spent most of my time with my older sister and brother since I was the "baby" of the family for the first ten years of my life. I enjoyed playing with my siblings because they took care of me and treated me like the baby girl. During the summers, before I was school-age, my brother and sister brought home their worksheets and workbooks full of Dick, Jane, Spot, Sally, and Puff. We played school all summer long. My sister and brother taught me how to read, write, and do simple arithmetic. When I entered kindergarten at age five, all the skills I learned became evident as my teachers saw my potential.

Juxtaposition, birth order, sibling affection, and a safe environment, were all at work!

Potential and possibilities are wrapped up within each child. Intellect, early access to curriculum, as constructed by my siblings, gave me a 'headstart' at school. It would be years later that this 'headstart' revealed it's true benefit. Entering the school community, ahead of the class, afforded me a rare opportunity. I was always the student during the summer school with my siblings and became the teacher's helper during the second grade in helping children who were having difficulties learning to read. Kudos to my siblings as my first teachers. These early experiences sparked my desire to enter the education profession.

Juxtaposition, access, acceptance, and acknowledgement of my potential, laid a firm foundation and platform of support as I set goals for my future.

I take time and opportunity to share my earliest educational experiences because it's the school community where we, as classmates, first crossed paths. I met some of you at Wagner Junior High School. This was my first experience, learning in the same space, with peers who didn't look like me. I encountered the rest of you at the Philadelphia High School for Girls. As a child, I lived in a segregated neighborhood, attended a segregated school and a segregated church. My interactions with Caucasian people were limited to shopping excursions with my mother or going to the neighborhood corner store where the proprietor was white. I have an aunt, from the Netherlands, but distance prevented any true interaction with her during my formative years. Segregated by race, religion, wealth, and ethnicity, my four years at Girls' High were consistently the same until juxtaposition and opportunity sparked a friendship.

I cannot recall the exact circumstances that began the relationship, but Lois and I became friends. In school and out of school, friends. Sharing excursions in the community and in our homes, friends. Sharing our future, hopes, and dreams, friends. Fifty years later, acknowledging we were young and stupid, friends. Grateful, fifty years later, that we can still call each other, friend!

Throughout my life, Church has been an integral piece of my identity. Faith in God and belief in His principles, have guided me day by day. This doesn't mean I always followed sound instruction. What it does mean, is at times I was successful, in spite of myself. The Black Church was a place where Blackness was celebrated, not beaten, as I saw on the evening news. Black leaders in the Church and community began to demand equal rights and access to a better quality of life for Black people. As I matured in faith, study, and understanding of biblical principles, Faith became my ark of safety.

Juxtaposition, community affirmation, and role models aligned to assist me in attaining my goals.

As I fast forward some fifty-five plus years from admittance to GHS in 1964, I continue on this journey of adding days and chapters to my life. I continue to lean on and glean strength from the building blocks of home, school, community, friendship, and faith. My years at GHS helped place my future on a path of success. I achieved many of the aspirations I shared with my friend, Lois. Looking back and committing a snippet of my journey in print is a daunting task. In the ever-present light of this pandemic, I'm being stretched to achieve a new dimension - author - as I prepare this piece for posterity.

This pandemic has highlighted the divide between the haves and have-nots. This pandemic has brought the daily challenges of those who live with housing insecurity, food insecurity, limited access to a basic quality education, and healthcare insecurity, into the limelight of the evening and cable news. This pandemic has brought issues of policing, institutional racism, and social justice into the conscious-ness of some, while affirming the reality of the situation for others. Personally, this pandemic has given me the gift of time. Time to pursue interests left simmering on the back burners or buried beneath doubt. As I think of you, the women of the 212, this pandemic has helped forge another link in our friendship chain. Friends with some of the most accomplished, interesting, and intriguing women with whom my path has crossed again.

Pre-Pandemic, I became intrigued with you, the women of the 212, as we shared our Facebook posts following our 40th Class Reunion. As we reached out individually, friendships ensued! Our commonalities, hopes, and aspirations are intertwined with our past, present and hopes for the future. We know we don't exist in a vacuum. We know we may be physically isolated and our fears shine through as a pity party takes center stage. Yet, we also know there's a group of women on whose virtual shoulder we can cry. Other than family, because we don't want to upset them with our tears and fears. By choice, this group of women, with the common bond of GHS 212, exists, determined to be there for one another. Our shared experience, then and now, is an unparalleled, unscripted part of us!

I told myself I wasn't going to name names; you know who you are! Ladies who respond to my impromptu phone calls, lunch and dinner invites. I'm grateful for every eager "yes" from: Jane, Val, Elaine, Ruth B, Diana, Nona, Robin, Sylvia, Kate, Paula G, Ellen, Ikelyn, Candy, Jackie, Gail, Paula, Anita, Kat, Starr, Theresa M, Gwen, Gwen B, Lois, Sandy, Susan, Gloria, and virtual Ladies of the 212, yearning to know more about our shared bonds. I've always equated interaction and shared experiences as a segue to friendship. You, women of the 212, will forever exist in my heart as a golden thread, intertwined and shining ever so brightly every time I think about you individually and collectively.

This pandemic has increased my heart's capacity to love and express my appreciation for each day and each shared experience. You are forever part of my identity. This pandemic has taken much and yet given more. As I consider its impact upon my life, I choose to align my days with hope and love. We, who are fortunate enough to have a choice, let's endeavor to keep hope shining into the darkness. Let's endeavor, the more, to help those in need. I'm determined to do what I can while I can. Juxtaposition plus identity plus love equals hope, forever, shining brightly.

Peace out!

"Vincit qui si vincit"

Riverdale, FL
February 2021

Emily Kahn, Julie Gabis, and 'Janie' Pearl were girlfriends before starting at Girls' High.

Emily Kahn-Freedman

TRYING TO CONNECT

WHEN I BRING TO MIND MY YEARS AT GIRLS' HIGH, what I experience first is discomfort. My discomfort was in part due to my age, as I was (and still am!) a year younger than most of you, having sped through Masterman Junior High on the accelerated track. I felt like a child compared to the rest of you, especially in 9th grade! In addition, there was discomfort in my body (too tall, nose too big, hair too curly, clothes not right), discomfort with the other girls (I didn't know how to join conversations, how to make friends), discomfort in my fear and belief that I would never have a boyfriend. (I always wanted to blame Girls' High for that, despite the evidence of other girls waiting for their Central High School boyfriends to meet them at the bottom of those big front steps.)

The only time I remember feeling that I "fit in" somewhere was in our senior year, when my best friends Connie Bernard and Margie Novack and I co-authored, produced, and directed our senior class show, "The Tangible Spirit." (Over 50 years later, as I drove with Connie back to Bethesda from our reunion, we spent most of the trip laughing hysterically as she tried to read the script aloud! Thank you, Margit, for having saved a copy!) That play, based on our favorite show "Star Trek," was the way I first got to know many of you. And I apologize, so very belatedly, to anyone who was hurt or offended by anything I did as producer or director or whatever my title was.

My other effort to fit in was also through drama. I was in some kind of drama class or club at Girls' High (was it after school?), where I met

Lily Samuel and Fran Nachman, as well as a girl from the 211, Prudy, whose younger brother turned out to be Kevin Bacon! Even more important to me was the opportunity to join the Central Drama Club, led by the incomparable, though sexist Mr. Rosenbaum (who later, sadly, died of AIDS). Being part of a play is the ultimate in experiencing teamwork and camaraderie. I met and tried to flirt with some boys, only realizing years later that my favorite "crushes" had been gay all along. And I remember trying to petition Dr. Thompson to allow us to attend Central for drama class, since Girls' High didn't offer a drama major.

I also tried to fit in with the cool "art girls" by auditing an art class, where I worked for a whole year on a very ugly wood sculpture. There I met and admired Susan Dukow and the late Diane Sisko, among others.

I guess I fit in most easily with the academically inclined girls in some of my classes.

They worked as hard for their grades as I did, but the "A"s didn't really help me feel good about myself. Somehow, I believed that the girls I didn't know as well were better, prettier, more confident, more interesting. They seemed to have the confidence I lacked, though only 40 to 50 years later did I learn that wasn't necessarily the case.

I'm going to skip through the entire next 52 years, which were as complex and as boring to talk about as anyone's. I'll only say the obvious, that the years have taught me a lot, and I'm still learning. Not ready to "graduate" just yet!

I have found some workable ways to connect with others. I've married (after false starts too numerous and embarrassing to mention) and raised two gifted and beautiful daughters. I've found a profession (marriage and family therapist) in which my whole job is to connect with people, and I've learned how to do that better than I'd thought I could. Even on Zoom. I've been active in the Jewish community since moving to Santa Fe – currently my synagogue volunteer work, also all on Zoom, takes up much more time than my spouse would like. (One of the women on the Temple Board with me, Marlene Kaplan Schwalje, was actually a member of the 213!) I've begun to feel at home here, especially through those Jewish community connections.

I've also learned that what I sensed at Girls' High is true – being "smart" isn't worth much compared to being able to connect with people. And as I suspected even then, some of the most interesting Girls' High classmates I've now met or re-met were not in my "star" or "AP" classes. Not to mention that many of the most successful women produced by the 212 were not in those classes, either. I've also learned that many of the girls I admired most were in fact not feeling so good about themselves at the time. That racism, sexism, family dysfunction and abuse were huge obstacles to many of the women I'm now getting acquainted with. That I was, and still am, very fortunate as well as very privileged.

But that despite it all, Girls' High managed to spit out the brilliant, gifted, loving, tough, hilarious and ageless women that I'm so glad to be connected with now.

Santa Fe, NM
February 2021

Wendy Keene
(aka Anaiis Salles)

IT'S VALENTINE'S DAY 2021.

I'm looking out at a dull gray wintry day. Snow on the ground. Quiet. And I'm thinking about what it was like to attend Philadelphia High School for Girls in the 1960s, and what it's like now to reflect on that experience in the following six decades.

We're in year two of the Covid-19 pandemic. I've been fortunate. The pandemic has had very little effect on my personal life. I was infected in October of 2019, and in three weeks, with intense holistic measures, I recovered. Yesterday, it was announced that Congo has admitted to another outbreak of Ebola virus. So... does the world currently have the financial resources or the will and determination to conquer Ebola - again? Or will the powers that be finally achieve their goal of clearing the African continent of the millions of people who stand in the way of all of those... resources.

Millions of Americans, and many abroad, are out of work because of the pandemic - restaurants, bars, hairdressers, the list is long - and the alcoholics are in an uproar - the cost of being inebriated is much higher and more visible. Many struggle with life being so quickly and suddenly thrown back to the old days before public education. The years before we sent our children off to school each day for others to enrich or infect their minds.

Women, mothers, grandmothers, sisters and aunts are picking up the lion's share of having daily family life turned upside-down and inside-out; more fear - less help.

The second impeachment of former president Donald J. Trump concluded only yesterday. Trump was, of course, acquitted - no one was surprised by that. The deal being struck was patently obvious. The political intelligentsia of the United States struck an uncomfortable compromise - let's hold Trump accountable in public theater and let's get on with the institutional business of finding a way through this global health, financial, housing, and educational debt bubble.

Detailed information about the January 6th, 2021 insurrection went into the national archives and will become part of the historical record of a president who would be king. By the end of day yesterday, Trump's attorney finally used the words 'violent insurrection'. And Lord help us, Mitch McConnell showed just how Machiavellian his underbelly really is as well as the unique skill of being of two minds within oneself. McConnell voted for acquittal and then disavowed Trump in a post proceedings statement. Unbelievable... unprecedented... and yet now part of the record.

If you are a person who is thinking about the future and who is choosing to move forward in the United States, as I am, this can't be done without appreciation for what's past. In the 1960s at Philadelphia High School for Girls, we were being educated to believe in - as being real - and to reach for - as being desirable - racial equality and inclusion. We were taught to reach for our own personal power as women, whatever color or race, or whatever our talents and interests may have been then. We were taught to reach toward these possibilities and to do so with a spirit of excellence, and do it with that 'Girls' High' spirit.

For many of my classmates, attending this school for academic excellence that drew its student body from throughout the city of Philadelphia, being a student there was a kind of a four-year petri dish akin to being part of a sorority, which never appealed to me; I've always been a loner. Although I enjoyed the company of many of my fellow students and found them remarkably talented, intelligent, bright, witty, funny and entertaining I became really close to only a few. One of these was Abigail Kaplan. Had she not moved to Chevy Chase, Maryland for her junior year, and had she remained in Philadelphia and stayed at

Girls' High, Abby would have graduated with our 212 class. Abby was my best friend, and we didn't let distance unravel our bond. Unfortunately, Abby died at the age of nineteen, shortly after attending the last anti-war demonstration in New York.

That was the Mayday demonstration. During the demonstration, Abby was clubbed on the back of the head by a policeman and knocked unconscious. She was taken to hospital for observation overnight and released the next day after having been medically assessed that she was fine.

After May, once on summer break from Bard College, Abby came to visit me and see her godson, Seth, my first child. Abby and I were still best friends. She's one of the most remarkable women of any age and of any stripe that I've ever known. She came to visit in June. It was nearly the second anniversary of my marriage to my high school sweetheart. Abby had driven her VW van to Bucks County, where we lived at the time with the intention to outfit the "bus" for a long-haul trip across the country with another friend of hers from Bard. This was how they were going to spend the summer.

After spending a few wonderful days together, including Abby putting my hand on the back of her head to feel the bump where she'd been clubbed, Abby left our house on Thursday. I had a bit of a premonition. There was something new, light-filled and truly stunningly beautiful about her. I thought she might have fallen in love with someone, but she assured me, no, this wasn't the case. As she drove away down our long country lane driveway, I knew I would never see her again. Saturday, the call came in that she had collapsed and subsequently died in Coudersport, Pennsylvania. Eventually, it was disclosed that she had died of a subdural hematoma, an undiagnosed result of being clubbed on the head by the cop in the New York city demonstration.

Abby died of a blood clot on the brain, like Officer Sicknick died from a blow to the head from a protester hitting him with a fire extinguisher on January 6 at the Capitol. Abby, too, had intervened to protect someone else in the crowd. The cop who clubbed her unconscious was going after that person and Abby intervened, putting her body in between them so the cop beat Abby instead.

It was an act of heroism, and the kind of great generosity that she shared. It's interesting to reflect on this today as I'm writing this on a deadline to get this little piece included into our writing group project centered on what it's like to be a 212er after all these years.

So, I begin with this connection to my time at Girls' High because our class was aware that the stakes for us were going to be very high. 212ers had come through the assassination of John F. Kennedy. This happened the year before attending Girls' High when I was still in junior high and a student at Masterman. This national spurt of social violence was followed by the murders of Rev. Martin Luther King, Jr. and Malcolm X. During our four-year stint at Philadelphia High School for Girls, 212ers were deeply impacted by the tragic death of one of our classmates who we were led to believe by her being found in the way she was on school campus that she allegedly committed suicide after it was determined that she had cheated on an exam. This happened at school during the school day, and this event was incredibly distressing for all of us. Abby was still in school with us at that time. I believe we were sophomores. Sherrie was President of our class. She was so popular, so bright, so intense. Why on earth did she not have the inner stamina to withstand that kind of stain on her character in her time at our high school?

We all had our traumas. I had a trauma that, while it didn't upend me completely psychologically to the point of wanting to kill myself, it did, result in my completely faltering on my ambition to be a writer. After being humiliated in front of English class by being accused of plagiarism for a short story that I'd written, I stopped writing. That charming episode was thanks to Mrs. G, who is now long dead. I actually still have a picture of her in my little snapshot book from some of our high school days. I have a picture of Abby, too, thankfully.

What was interesting, was at that time, the most serious thing that I believe we weren't actually talking about - was this sort of permeation of energies in our class that moved through us like an inner atmosphere - we were confronting the issues of racial inequality and inclusion. We were confronted with our academic goals and how well we were able to adapt and develop as students. We were being confronted with how able and prepared we were to find a way to fully mine our innate talents and interests, which for me included art and music, and had included the aspiration to be a writer up to that misadventure with Mrs. G.

We had not yet arrived at the tap turned full on about to flood in era of feminism - symbolized by the bold choice to not wear a bra and to not absorb without question the moral edicts of our mothers – to keep nickels between our knees and our panties on - because we were the first generation of young, menstruating women to have access to the birth control pill.

We knew how to network that information in our class. I networked that with a few of my fellow students and made an appointment with a center city, female gynecologist, who, being a feminist herself, understood the real entrapment anguish of an unwanted pregnancy. Some of the girls in our class ended up trapped in that way, but some of us didn't.

I got on the pill. I remember in our conversation the doctor and I being very clear. She asked, "Do your parents know that you're doing this?" I replied, "Absolutely not. My parents don't talk to me about what they do in their bedroom. Why am I going to talk to them about what I'm doing with my sexual life?" At age fifteen, this was my confident response; I considered us equals.

What I was sure of was that I was interested in finding out about my sexuality. I had a steady boyfriend, and we were interested in finding out about our sexuality together as a couple. So, this energy of getting a handle on our sexual energy and well-being was permeating through our years at Girls' High. I don't know who of my sisters in our 212 class can remember any of that, or came close to that, or went into that, or had a brush with that, or how many just took on the good girl ethic and edict that was part of the whole "Girls' High Girls" mystique.

A very interesting time; politically, socially, and culturally - very demanding. Lots and lots and lots of change bordering on transformation. We were ushered through four years of those pressures and those trans-formations. Then we were launched with the hope - I think that the faculty at the school really did hope - Oh God, Dr. Thompson! I can't remember our principal's name. At this point, I no longer have my yearbook. Some women do have their yearbooks which I find fascinating.

But I do remember the energy in classes, in the halls, and in assem-bly was somewhere between Vestal Virgin, librarian, and armed forces volunteer females – WAVES, or WACs or whatever those female recruits were called during the war – where you took up your duty and you nursed or supported the troops and this was an expression of your empowered femininity. How do you support men first and use the leftover crumbs to fashion something for yourself?

We were absolutely being encouraged to consider a different path. We were encouraged to try to find the balance, if at all possible, between crafting lives in which we could fully flower and blossom into what we wanted to as regards the standard roles of wife, mother, daugh-ter - whatever.

I'm thinking about this today; and the political turmoil that we lived through then. The Vietnam War. Then sitting through the impeachment of Richard Nixon. I watched every second of the entire televised process. I remember being so elated and joyful when Nixon finally recognized that he was going to have to resign. I recall feeling aghast at his political maneuvers whereupon Gerald Ford immediately pardoned Nixon. So, this week has been a flashback. Nixon. Clinton. Trump. Thank goodness for Carter and Obama. Reagan's presidency, administration, and policies actually laid the foundation for the events of January 6th, 2021

This Valentine's Day, the upper echelons of intelligentsia, the Harvard grads, the Yale grads and Stanford grads, these ivory towers and bastions of white male intelligentsia, intellectual privilege in law, and sci-ence, and in all of the intellectually inspired social manipulation that have followed as a shadow from our time in our association with the British government, most notably the Tavistock Institute? These forces are all hedging their bets that they will continue to control the future of humanity.

Then, of course, we had come of age with the Beatles just as technology was making its huge and relentless incursion into the collective psyche. I feel almost breathless by the amount of life that we have been force-fed in just a few decades. Now, we are in another era of force-fed change because it is our children - and hopefully we can help our children who are adults now themselves and who have to steward their children - and with Goddess' grace, our grandchildren and future generations will figure out how and if human beings can survive on this planet now that it has been fatally strip-mined by the greed of capitalism and empire.

I watched in amazement as Donald Trump - I don't even know what to call him, he careens precariously between being a one man circus act and a carnival huckster - yet he's seen as a legitimate person. He's an illegitimate businessman. He's cheated people out of enormous amounts of money. He's defrauded people of millions. Trump University? It goes on and on and on and on and on, but it is damaging to me that those who have been effectively brainwashed - using Tavistock Institute technique, and communications technique, and wordsmithing technique, and sound design technique, and movie technology and television commercial technique, that about half of the American population of voting age has been completely socially engineered to feel - it's all about creative emotional energy being funneled by experts - that this man was somehow going to make America great again while what I observed was the reincarnation of Hitler.

Wasn't hard to see. So, I'm grappling with those emotions, with my perceptions, and with my grasp of history. The long and little of it is global, cultural transformation sponsored the incredible struggle of people of color. Mind you, people of color make up the majority of the world's population. Three-quarters of the world's population is non-white yet through the machinations of social engineering at the behest of institutions like the Tavistock Institute and its very, very successful approach to social engineering, the illusion of racial inferiority and racism has spread all over the world: another global pandemic for which there is no vaccine.

We have, in America for more than 400 years, been carrying the burden of genetic inferiority and superiority on our backs. Donald Trump is - other than the slave-holders of the days before the Civil War - the embodiment of that kind of white patriarchal, completely narcissistic, clearly psychopathic, and totally oblivious to his own racism, a power icon as testified to by the people who have unfortunately had to be in close dealings with him.

These are people who still possess remnants of conscience and memory, of being compassionate and having a sense of humanity. These people have borne witness and in both impeachment trials Trump threw his own under the bus, as he consistently did for all four years of his presidency.

I am in a state of astonishment because this is the through-line - it's a direct through-line from the Republican side of the aisle - beginning with the assassination of JFK and moving steadily forward - on adhering to their God-given agenda that America is for white people.

And I'm astonished by this. I'm not directly affected by it because I'm not brainwashed (studies have determined that it's more challenging to fully brainwash people of color). However, I've lived through it. I see the results of it. I'm very fortunate to live in a community that is heart first and mind second, which is the balance that allows one to maintain one's humanity and compassion.

So, I wanted to share that today. I think it's interesting in terms of how our 212 class of women has had these transformations and backlashes wash through our personal lives. Whatever professional lives we've crafted for ourselves and how we used our academic privilege to make different choices as we come of age at the beginning of an era shaped to respect individual choice over religious dogma and cultural tradition.

This is the perspective from which I choose to contribute. This is my piece/peace.

I extend a heartfelt congratulations to all of us in the 212 Class from the Philadelphia High School for Girls. To those still alive, to those we fondly remember, to those who are still healthy, to those who have gone through trials and tribulations with health challenges and professional challenges, I congratulate us for being willing to turn our lenses in so many new directions. Hats off to focusing on our experiences, realizing and appreciating the enormous privilege that this particular educational opportunity and challenge generated for all of us; whatever we have done with this privilege, we have done.

I would like to congratulate us for somehow having had enough sense of ourselves as women to apply ourselves to a new vision of who we might be and become, and to include academic excellence as part of that journey. How a serious focus on academics was part of moving us forward to find a way – to include being a secretary if that's what we wanted, or an office worker, or domestic, or a woman who owned a cleaning business, or a woman who earned a law degree, or a woman who earned a medical degree - into many unimagined possibilities.

We had choice; we were a privileged group of young women who, however luck and hard work and circumstances conspired with us, came together at Girls' High to go on to contribute to the world we live in.

Happy Valentine's Day to you all! I congratulate you.

I congratulate myself, too for having survived the Chinese curse: "May you live in interesting times."

Philadelphia, PA
February 2021

Marsha Kramer Prosini

LOST AND FOUND

AS I GROW OLDER, I REALIZE THAT OVER TIME I WILL lose people I love and have known for a good part of my life.

I was prepared for her death when my mother died 9 days before she reached 101 years old.

I was somewhat prepared for the close friend that died at 81 from COVID-19 after she spent a large part of her life in a wheelchair with only the use of one hand because of MS.

I was not prepared to lose two close friends at the age of 33. Both were bridesmaids at my first wedding. One was murdered by gunshot; the other was killed by cancer.

I was devastated to lose my lifelong best friend when we were 60. Friends for over 56 years. Some said it was like losing a sister. I thought it was worse. I didn't get to choose my sisters.

In 2020, during the quarantine, I spoke frequently to my friend of over 50 years. I was shocked to receive a text from her husband (he was unable to talk) that she had fallen down the basement steps in November. When she died two weeks later from severe head trauma, I was again devastated.

Why are four of my contemporaries gone from my life? Why them? Why not me?

According to my mother – and she was always right – when we are born, we have a date stamped inside of us which is when it is our time. It made as much sense as anything else. As my mom got older facing blindness and dementia, she told me that they made a mistake with her date. She always kept her sense of humor.

And so, life goes on if you are lucky enough. I am in disbelief that it has been over 52 years since my graduation from Girls' High. Time has a way of flying by and you can't stop it. Since our 40th reunion, and the establishment of our GHS Facebook page, I have had the joy of reuniting with old friends, some that go back as far as kindergarten. I have also found beautiful new friends that I never really knew in high school.

I'm so happy to have our 50th anniversary directory that Emily so wonderfully envisioned. It was an honor and fun to work on it with her. I was able to reach out to our awesome women with questions, or just to bug them to send us their bios. It is amazing to read what our class has accomplished. We have lost too many, and it is a reminder to the rest of us to appreciate our lives.

In October of 2019, I was diagnosed with breast cancer. Two of our classmates that are breast cancer survivors reached out to me. I can't tell you how much their support and knowledge helped me navigate the complexities and the decision-making process on my journey. There was additional support and prayers offered when I came forward on Facebook. I was lucky that my cancer was found early. I was also fortunate to have been able to complete my radiation treatments right before the quarantine began in Pennsylvania.

All of our lives changed drastically in 2020. There were some that were totally isolated and alone. There were some that were able to continue to work from home. There were some, like myself, that sought solitude because there were too many people in the house.

No matter what our situation, we were all brought together by one of our classmate's brilliant idea to have Zoom sessions. It was great to see everyone "live". Some attended all. I skipped those around elections because there was way too much political discussion and dissension at my house.

I have learned many personal lessons from our interactions. I never fully appreciated my childhood and my parents and sisters. I have heard of those that were abused, beaten or thrown out of their houses.

We also get to share each other's joys. The birth of a grandchild. The wedding of a son or daughter. New pets and funny dog and cat tricks. A move to a new home or downsizing to a different state. It's all good.

So, although I have experienced the loss of close friends, I have found old and new friends. I am truly grateful for that.

Warrington, PA
January 2021

Jackie Krenetz Dering

GROWING UP IN MT. AIRY ALMOST EVERYONE AROUND
me was Jewish. I remember being shocked when I was told that Jews
were a minority group. Almost every kid in school and all of our neighbors
were Jewish, after all. Arriving at Girls' High I was immediately amazed
at the wide variety of students from all parts of the city and many backgrounds. We had girls from South Philly who were raised Catholic; we
had girls from the Northeast; we had Black girls; we had a few girls from
Asian backgrounds. It was a wonderful wide diverse world. Of course,
we were all girls and all smart so maybe not as diverse as I thought, but
a wonderful base to grow on. We also had implicit feminism in everything
we were taught. We were expected to learn.

The most lasting gifts Girls' High gave to me were a broader world
view on which to build, an excellent education, and as it turns out, a fabulous group of women who would return to my life. I have never walked
into a room full of people and felt less educated or unsure of how to
speak. I have not felt uncomfortable surrounded by people from different
backgrounds from me. The quality of our education left us on par with
anybody at any college. Life is much easier when you feel free to ask
questions without fear of feeling stupid and when you feel confident that
your spoken language is correct and even that you sound so much better
in French than you really are. Thank you, Madame Bernstein.

The education we got went beyond sounding good. We learned
critical thinking in many of our classes. Special thanks to Mrs. Rubinstein
for that. In addition to being able to dissect literature we learned to look
beneath the surface. We argued economics and history and politics.
Thank you, Mrs. Kubert. And we learned math and science before it

became mainstream to make sure girls had these skills. I also learned that it was quite possible to fall through the cracks in even such an environment.

I was undiagnosed ADD and really struggled with paying attention and staying on topic. This is still difficult for me especially if I'm not so interested. I question why nobody wondered why I did so well on standardized tests, but not so well in many classes. I surely could have used an adult to take an interest. The adults fell short on other fronts as well. I remember telling Miss Deglin that I didn't want her to hug me and getting thrown out of class. The guidance counselor told me I needed to apologize. I wouldn't. This wouldn't happen today.

Our senior year 1967-1968 was world changing. We lost Martin and Bobby. These losses were devastating, but we didn't lose hope. Colleges were becoming bastions of activity. I learned from our Black sisters that life wasn't always as I thought and people had experiences and struggles far different from each other. I learned from our early hippies that there was fun and love to be had. I hope I learned to listen to other people. Senior year launched me into four years of political activism in college and beyond including getting arrested while picketing the White House protesting the Wage Freeze. The cops were just as unkind as they can be now. We were teargassed in the wagon for singing. We tried to keep singing, but that just didn't work out so well. I vividly remember the small metal toilet in the middle of the cell. As an adult I have worked on many campaigns and have worked to promote women candidates.

When I received the invitation to the 40th reunion my curiosity was piqued. I thought of many girls that I would like to see as women. Little did I know that I was about to acquire a new family of women. I arrived and before I even got out of the parking lot I immediately recognized many of the women walking toward the event. I felt so very happy to be there. For me it was a magical day. Old friendships were renewed and new friendships were begun with women I hadn't known in school. It was like meeting family members I hadn't met before but having an undeniable link with them. The bond was just magical. My classmates have been so very important to me especially during the exhausting past five years. In addition to psychological support and love I had acquired a group of women who as a group know just about everything. We were immediately each other's go to for information and advice.

Fast forward to the year of the Pandemic. My women as I often like to think of us have been present. We have held together through our Zoom calls and Facebook. We are more than friends. We can bicker and we can sympathize with each other. We are a family.

Hiding in the house for a year has been trying and boring and wasteful of our most limited resource, time. I am grateful that my son is well, to have my classmates, that my home is cozy, and my husband and I have weathered this year together and mostly that I am still here to write about it.

Swarthmore, PA
February 2021

Katherine LaMonaca Hanson

AS THE BEATLES ONCE WROTE, "THERE ARE PLACES
I'll remember, all my life, though some have changed. Some forever, not
for better, some have gone, and some remain". At seventy years of age,
tracing back in my mind to high school isn't the easiest of tasks. There is
certainly much I have forgotten, but the changes that contributed to who
I am today have, for better or for worse, remained.

I sometimes think of how I became a Girls' High Girl. How did I find
the courage to leave my South Philly neighborhood, the neighborhood
whose borders I barely left over my first fourteen years of life? How did
I leave my friends with whom I had attended St. Monica's Parochial
School and conspired with every day? How did I hop a bus to Broad
and Snyder to catch the subway to the other end of the city to attend
Philadelphia High School for Girls? I honestly wanted to stay with my
friends and attend St. Maria Goretti. However, my parents had different
plans for me. Their own education was limited. Neither of them held a
high school diploma. As blue-collar workers, they had struggled to keep
us in the middle class of society and understandably wanted better for
their children. I could have fought it, but I knew my Italian parents would
make my life miserable. Every mistake I would make would be greeted
with, "If only you had gone to Girls' High". It was better to concede than
retreat from what they had set in their minds.

I was a good, not a great student. What I had though, was a sister
who was an outstanding student and carried my last name to Girls' High
three years before me. I'm not certain, but I believe the one thing on the
entrance exam that got me past the door was our last name at the top of

the page. Seriously, after a few weeks with teachers who had my sister in their class, I heard the question, "So you're Adeline LaMonaca's sister?"

Sister aside, I forged my own way through Girls' High. I made friends from other walks of life and though academics didn't come easy, friendships did. My closest bond was with the other girls who rode that long subway ride. We later became known as "The Subway Girls". However, the friendships made with girls from outside my own culture opened my eyes to a wider view of what lay outside my narrow world. I attended my first bat mitzvah. I will always be grateful for the friendships I shared.

While I attended Girls' High, my neighborhood friends became closer to each other. Though they included me on weekend events, I could feel that we didn't have the close bond we had once held. I enjoyed activities with the girls I traveled to and from school each day. But when the four years ended, I felt a huge loss. There was no way to get back in with my old friends and now, once again, my new friends were old. As time passed, so did my time spent with them.

As I mentioned earlier, I was not a strong academic student. Thankfully, Philadelphia Community College was a great springboard for students like me. I continued my subway rides for two more years and it allowed me to mingle in the hustle and bustle of Center City, a place I always enjoyed. I had some great instructors at the college. They stretched my academics and I began to realize that I had absorbed more from Girls' High than I had imagined. I knew how to do research and how to put my thoughts onto paper. I began to understand that my ideas mattered. I could express them in front of my peers. I received better grades than I had at Girls' High and was totally ready when I entered Penn State's Elementary Education program in Middletown, Pa.

Attending Penn State in a small town is quite different from the experiences I had heard from those who went to the main campus at University Park. We didn't live in dorms but in small housing complexes. This allowed us more freedom from the watchful eyes of dorm monitors who checked rooms and made sure everyone was following the rules.

The first year, I managed to evade the drugs brought in by my three roommates; but it is in my nature to want to be accepted. So, by the second year, I was right in the circle inhaling marijuana and dropping acid. I became one of the gang. I have no one to blame but myself, because I am or I "was" who I "was" back then. I managed to stay on the Dean's list for my final two years and exited with a Bachelor's in Education. I exited the college with friendships as well.

With my degree, I returned to South Philly, moved back in with my parents, and took a teaching job at Bonsall Elementary School in Camden, New Jersey. Here is where I further broadened my experiences with other cultures. Thanks to Sandra Lewis, a strong and loving African American mentor, I grew as a primary teacher. I had the support of a community I came to love and respect. I always felt that they "had my back" and trusted me with their precious little ones. Fortunately/unfortunately, I fell in love with my future husband and left Bonsall after only three years.

In 1975, the USS Sampson Naval Fleet returned from a tour in Greece and brought to the Philadelphia Naval Base a handsome sailor named Ed Hanson. We were married a year later, and I still consider him a fine "catch" (pun intended).

In 1977, we moved to our current home in Vancouver, Washington where we raised two children and now enjoy life with our five grandchildren. While raising our children and teaching full time, I completed my Master's in Education at Washington State.

In 2013, I received an invitation to our 45th Class Reunion. It was perfect, because I had already made plans to fly home to Philadelphia a week before the reunion. The day after the reunion I took flight with my brilliant (LOL) sister and my cousin to take off on an adventure to Cefalu, Sicily where we would meet my mother's cousins for the first time. This is a magical story that I will reserve for another time.

During that forty-fifth reunion, I reminisced with the girls from my class who now had become women and found beautiful souls with wonderful stories to tell. I was sorry to see that weekend end, but happy for the promises made to keep in touch. For many of us, Facebook would be the vehicle that would bind us.

Another reunion in 2018, our fiftieth, strengthened more ties. But when Covid hit in the wicked year of 2020 we realized what our friendships truly meant. When Susan Dukow suggested, and then managed, our Zoom meetings, more and more 1968 alumni attended, not just to see the faces of our former classmates, but to have deeper conversations about our lives, past and present. Many of us who attend, have come to depend on these meetings to stay connected. Susan has done a sublime job of managing the boxes of faces and the voices that otherwise might be chaotic. During these calls, collectively and independently, women submit ideas to challenge the minds of our former classmates. Hence the reason this piece is being written. Yes, it's a stretch for me; but I did it and I look forward to more endeavors. Who knows what is brewing in the mind of one or more of these accomplished females?

Vancouver, WA
December 2020

When we unearthed classmates, we may have not known before, Gloria London was one of our treasures to behold. A fully realized woman of many talents, an archaeologist, seen here excavating in Jordan, and an artist who designed pieces for her mother who then put needle to point. The "Alphabet" seen here (you really must see it in color) was done by Elaine London in 1991. The brooch next to her initials, a piece that belonged to Gloria's grandmother Sarah German, was later attached.

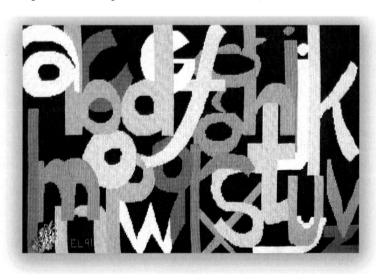

Gloria London

2020

IN JULY, 1968, ONE SHORT MONTH AFTER GRADUATING from Girls' High School, my family packed up everything and spent two weeks on a ship sailing for Israel. Once there, I studied archaeology and worked until 1980 when I relocated to Tucson (U of AZ) for a Ph.D. My time at GHS led me to believe that women could achieve anything, and in Israel, Prime Minister Golda Meir proved it to be so. My father, a WWII veteran, felt that a high school education was enough for girls. My mother knew otherwise. Philip London passed away in my junior year at Tel Aviv University, but support from the Veterans Administration enabled my three siblings and me to work our way through school and complete our studies (archaeologist, physician, chef, and lawyer). It was not easy.

During years of teaching and presenting invited lectures at college campuses across the U.S., I never met a professor who attended our all girls' school or any other Philly school other than Central High, the boys' school down the hill from GHS. The Philadelphia accent makes us immediately identifiable. Central produced a remarkable number of scientists, historians, and linguists compared to GHS. My thanks to members of our class who have taught at schools, universities, or colleges. Students need female role models and the encouragement they give to girls. At times I have been the sole female professor in a department or IN THE WHOLE SCHOOL. After the birth of my daughter, I decided to work from home and educate her while continuing to present lectures around the country and internationally.

While living in Israel, I met visiting 212ers (Leah H. and Meira W.) and the teacher of those infamously unsuccessful, experimental, waste-of-time French classes, who sat with her parents in a restaurant, at a table next to my family. The Tel Aviv encounter was not pleasant. Otherwise, ties to the class ended entirely until Emily K. found me online around 2012. I reconnected with Sandi H. at the 45th and then Cindy D. and Lily S. at the 50th reunion. But the 212 Zoom calls initiated by Susan D. opened up a whole new world of the past under the present pandemic.

Due to the virus, I have not been anywhere, other than neighborhood walks, since February 24, 2020. A neighbor returning from a visit to family in Taiwan described Covid-19 restrictions and limitations on movement there that had been mandatory since January. I began to follow those guidelines immediately. As a result of working from home for decades, the virus causes little change in my daily life. I resolutely continue to analyze data from my excavations of ancient sites and my ethno-archaeological fieldwork observing traditional potters in Jordan, Cyprus, and the Philippines.

My book, published in April, 2020, Wine Jars and Jar Makers of Cyprus: The Ethnoarchaeology of *Pitharia*, is slowly leaving the storeroom. The pandemic delayed its distribution, but positive comments from readers began to arrive in November. A new book about ancient pottery excavated at Jezreel, in northern Israel, comes out shortly. Will it meet the same fate – stuck in boxes? My next monograph, about coil-built pottery still made by female potters in Cyprus, advances nicely because: 1) it is better than cleaning; 2) gardening is challenging in the Seattle rain and cold; and 3) I already wrote postcards for voters in Georgia.

A favorite research topic concerns the role of ancient women. Quite simply, they did it all – the backbreaking work, nurturing, healing, educating, etc. Male archaeologists write that ancient women were mothers, prostitutes, cooks, and water carriers who met to gossip at the well. In reality, before filling and carrying that heavy jug, they exchanged vital information that sustained the entire community. Women safeguarded knowledge about natural methods to soothe and heal the youngest and oldest segments of society or to recognize and treat childhood illnesses. More than medical experts, they preserved traditions, rituals, heritage, and specialized information, such as recipes for foods enjoyed by all. Women have always been teachers and guardians of tradition.

One positive outcome of the pandemic involves the walks with a neighbor and her two dogs, instead of going solo on a longer steeper walk. I need someone to talk to. Zoom meetings with 212ers are a second, positively wonderful development. Even a lack of negative outcomes turns into a positive: my brother-in-law did not contract Covid from his girlfriend. Both teach high school in Holland. At least one of their colleagues has succumbed to the virus.

My recent graduate (California Institute of Technology, 2020) is thankfully at home; she has a post-doctoral fellowship at Cornell University. Palma came back to Seattle in August after learning that she would have no office or contact with anyone on campus in New York at Cornell. Her father happily stays home and teaches theoretical physics via Zoom. The pandemic means that they no longer indulge me with Friday night dinner guests. Palma's research continues online and she is content not to go anyplace. Her current research involves creating a mathematical model to efficiently eliminate debris that floats in outer space. She has also joined the ranks of sourdough overproducers. The house smells great from the baking, but she and I have been gluten free for 24.5 years.

Thanks to the 212 Zooms, I learned that Fran Y. remembers when I had my ears pierced in 8th grade. We shared a table in a science lab during homeroom. Maybe the piercings gave her the misimpression that I was "cool". Not true. My mother told my sister (GHS 213) and me to get into the car for a doctor's appointment. Throughout the tense car ride we had no idea why we needed a doctor. Turns out it was for ear piercing. Fran, was it because of the pierced ears that you called me at home to talk about boys? "You mean the boys in our junior high school class?" I asked. "NO! The dreamy boys". "I have no idea what you mean," I responded.

At age 38, when university officials informed me that I had chosen to become a professor rather than create a family, I knew that was not my decision. Marriage followed in 1989. Most female archaeologists our age who excavate in the Near East are unmarried and/or childless. To excavate every summer requires leaving the kids behind, which most men do easily. Today, more women take their kids to digs, as some men have done for decades. Nowadays, when invited to contribute a chapter to a book or participate in a panel, I agree only if it includes a reasonable representation of women.

It is incredibly rewarding to reconnect with 212ers to create new friendships and cherish former acquaintances. However, the gulf between girls of color and everyone else was large in the 1960s and remains ever-present. Five decades later, please let 212 classmates bridge the divide.

At the 45th reunion I was disappointed to see tables of either Black or White girls seated for lunch. Of course, we all like to be with those we know best. Later at the reunion, when we lit a candle for those who had passed away that year, I stood to light one in memory of Margo Brown. The Black girls who rose at the same time looked at me with some curiosity. I felt compelled to explain my presence at the table, as if I was intruding. Did I make an error in judgement in my first meeting with classmates after 45 years? Had I been away from Philly too long to realize that entrenched divisions between Blacks and Whites persist? Maybe Seattle, Tucson, and the rest of the world are too progressive for Philadelphians? Was this a moment for the Black sisters to shine in memory of "one of their own"? Should I have stayed seated? After mentioning that I had known Margo since Wagner Jr. High School, I received a nice long hug from Paula G. If we did not sit together, at least we could mourn the passing of a classmate who was not fortunate enough to share the same space.

The city of Philadelphia, with its two huge rivers, endless parks, and abundance of historical sites marking the birth of this country, remains part of my past. Until I planned a stopover during the 45th reunion, the only purpose of going home involved cemetery visits. Hence, after the reunion I headed straight back to my research in Cyprus, a divided island in the Mediterranean. Although most Cypriots yearn for reunification, current regional conflicts enable surrounding countries to decide its fate. In the U.S.A. we get to decide to sit where we like. We choose our friends.

If it remains hard for some classmates to acknowledge, yet forgive, the injustices and the divisions of the past, how can the country ever come together? Please, let GHS 212 be the role model in recognizing and rejecting the unfairness and injustice of our history including the on-going risks that POC contend with in their homes or on city streets and highways. As teenagers in high school, none of our brains had fully developed. We were still young, malleable, and too often prone to follow the pervasive unjust and unequal practices that permeated 1960s society. Please forgive those of us who hardly had any inkling of what it means to be Black in the U.S.A.

Seattle, WA
November 2020
http://faculty.washington.edu/london/g/index.html
Women Potters of Cyprus (*video*)
https://www.youtube.com/watch?v=2LVclOlHTBg

Arlene Margolis Slepchik

GIRLS' HIGH GIRL

HERE I AM, ALMOST 70, AND HERE WE ARE REMINISC-
ing on the impact of having attended Girls' High. A serious, academic high school with lots of pressure to succeed and beat the girl sitting next to you in assembly. Clearly, anyone who went there was bright, but what did that actually mean?

A serious, academic high school with rigorous demands. Truthfully, I didn't fit in anywhere, starting with my life at home. I did not have a regular, 'normal' family, as I was raised by my aunt and my grandmother, joined by a grandfather for a short period of time. My mom was never well enough to take care of me, and I did not meet her until I was in kindergarten, for short periods of time. I became a very serious, hard-working, diligent student, as my sole desire was to go away to college, which I knew would only be possible through full scholarships. I studied a lot and was always worried it was never enough. My family did not want me to leave the house, despite the fact they understood it was the best thing for me. I had some close friends, but never shared what happened in my house and rarely invited them over. I do remember since we couldn't afford a sweet sixteen, my dear friends Carol Lipkin, Susan Dudnick and Nancy Feldman invited me downtown for a lovely lunch and bought me a beautiful purse. I only remember kindness and support from my dear friends.

I seemed to have a flare for languages, especially thanks to Miss Beck (Camus and Sartre in senior year) and Miss MacCorkell. I arrived well prepared for university. I have still maintained my love of reading, literature and cultural events until this day. I volunteer at the Jewish public library here in Montreal, and am an active member of the English Cultural Committee. I knew how to study, how to do academic research, how to write a paper. These are the skills I went to university with, thanks to Girls' High.

Early on at Fairleigh Dickinson University, I was placed in senior level advanced French classes, followed by independent studies, adding Russian to my repertoire, and in junior year, wrote my first thesis. The head of the language department had planned an excellent grad school program for me, and had high hopes for my career. But of course, real life intervened, as it often does. My mother died suddenly, horribly, which seriously impacted my life. I wound up transferring to university in Montreal, to live in a French environment and be with my then boyfriend, now husband, of almost fifty years. I've always felt my serious habits, starting in high school, along with my family life, steeled me for what was, and what was still to come.

I became the French professor in an elementary school, before starting my own family. In retrospect, that's what I wanted all along, a regular family. We have three healthy children (now adults) who have made their own choices in life. I feel that's what we gave them - the independence to be who and what they wanted, something not available to me.

Prior to my 50th birthday, I had a tremendous shock. I developed a rare, autoimmune disease which took over my life for twelve years. I became a medical experiment for my doctor, and came down with other rare diseases, such as histoplasmosis, as well as being hospitalized with shingles, so severe, that my own physician did not recognize me. I have continued to be a medical oddity. I feel sometimes everything that came before allowed me to survive what happened to me.

Often the pain was worse than the disease. I consider myself to be exceptionally lucky to be still standing alongside my amazing husband. Surprisingly, we have made some extraordinary trips and seen incredible sights that I never could imagine, especially when you consider I spent a long time as a blind woman. Thanks to my doctor, my vision is excellent.

I don't know what awaits us in the future, but I hope we will stay healthy during this pandemic. Considering the Trump presidency, I know I am fortunate to live in Montreal. Watching the United States disintegrate has been heartbreaking. I wish Biden lots of luck and hope that he and Kamala Harris stay safe. This week watching the inauguration was the first time I felt any degree of happiness regarding the U.S. in a very long time.

And I must say a genuine thank you to everyone who wrote about their experiences. I found them very moving and was shocked to hear many were as nervous as I was as a high school student. A huge surprise! I felt it was important to contribute. Thank you to everyone who participated, and to Susan and Ellen for encouraging us and organizing it.

Montreal, Quebec
January 2021

Patricia Anne McDonnell

PERFECT LITTLE LADY

RAISED BY A SINGLE MOM, I NEVER HAD A FATHER AS part of my life. He spent much of his time gambling and was never able to hold a steady job because he was so unreliable. As a result, my Mom had to support us. She worked full-time, and I stayed with a babysitter. My early childhood years were spent with adults. When I was about three-years old, I went to nursery school. I vaguely remember the other children and had very little interaction with them. It was always just my Mom and me. I was so well behaved that she was able to take me everywhere. Her friends and my family adored me. I was the perfect little lady. At home I could amuse myself for hours with my beloved dolls and my books.

We moved to West Oak Lane when I was five-years old. The schools were excellent, and my Mom hoped that I would eventually attend Girls' High. We lived in a small duplex apartment in a very nice Jewish neighborhood. Everyone was friendly and looked out for us. Although I was extremely self-conscious around children my age, I did meet two little girls, only because my Mom asked them to play with me. They often inquired about my father, and eventually they realized, "Patricia doesn't have a father."

Adults never asked me about my father, but children are different. They are curious, but for me it was uncomfortable because I felt as if I didn't fit in with the others. I did have a wonderful childhood, though, and my Mom tried to instill confidence in me with ballet, Girl Scouts, Bible school, Church choir, and ice skating in the winter. On my sixth birthday she bought me my first pet, a little green parakeet. I named him Chipper. He was so delightful, and I felt this overwhelming sense of love for him. When I uncovered his cage each morning, he greeted me with sweet chirping sounds. He would sit on my shoulder, perch on my finger, and give me kisses. I even taught him to talk. Chipper made me so happy. He was my very special friend. Life was perfect.

Summers were spent with my Aunt Florence and Uncle Park in Birchrunville, a small historic village located in West Vincent Township in northern Chester County, Pennsylvania. Everyone called me Tootsie, even well into my twenties. Aunt Florence and I swam in the creek, and sometimes I slept outside in a "tent" made from sticks and a blanket. There were no other children. We walked to the general store for the mail (It was also the Post Office), and to buy fresh meat and produce. Sometimes we used the pay phone to call my Mom. I went on all kinds of imaginary adventures riding my "make pretend" horse, Fury. I played Wagon Train and amused myself with my paper dolls from the Sears catalog. Every year we went to the Kimberton Fair, where we went on the amusement rides, played the arcades to win stuffed animals, and ate cotton candy. My other Aunt owned a dairy farm a short distance away. I loved the farm animals, feeding the chickens, playing with the piglets, the precious litters of kittens, and her collie, Lad. I was happy and free. Nobody made fun of me. I was everyone's Tootsie.

Then I turned thirteen-years old; I was no longer a little lady. I was a teenager in every sense. The dolls were replaced by boys and the Beatles. I lost my baby fat, and with my long "Summer Blonde" hair the kids in the neighborhood stopped calling me "Porky". I had a Jewish boyfriend from Central, and I was ready for Girls' High.

With my babysitting money, I was able to buy Ladybug and Villager clothes, a John Romaine initial handbag, and wear Weejuns. My close friends called me "Patti Segal". I was officially a Mt. Airy Jewish girl. As I wandered the pink marble hallways, I was incognito. The other students knew me from classes, but I was never in a clique because I was friendly with everyone. I never fit into the mold of a typical Girls' High girl. I never carried a "stupid" bookbag, never washed my gymsuit, and I detested singing those French, Spanish, German, and Latin Christmas carols in the auditorium. I never went to Prom. I had no enthusiasm for Contest. It surely wasn't like having a football team to cheer for in a co-ed school. Perhaps the Girls' High tradition was not for me. Academically, I did excel at Math and Science. English literature was about reading the "Cliff Notes". French was about studying the English translation of "Les Miserables". I just didn't like to conform to anything. I did, however, receive excellent grades, but I kept that to myself because nobody likes a person who is "too smart".

My greatest attribute was my sense of humor, which was probably my coping mechanism for feeling different. It didn't really matter though, because someone would come up with a goofy idea, and I would go for it. When we were voting for our class President, we were permitted to write in names other than those who were officially nominated. I thought it would be funny to write in a fictitious person to see if anyone would vote for her. I nominated Bessi Katz. When the final votes were tallied, she was on the ballot. My crazy friends actually voted for her. But sadly, in the end, she received only a few votes. Nobody ever bothered to check. I liked getting away with funny pranks and amusing others with my antics. In the end, I graduated wearing my very short white dress, white patterned pantyhose and cute white babydoll shoes. My Mom wasn't thrilled about the too-short dress, but she was proud of me, and in a way, I guess I was too. Perhaps, it is not about fitting in, it is about finding your way.

Fast forward to our 40th reunion. For me it was completely unremarkable. I only knew a few people and had very little in common with the others. Sometime in 2008, I joined Facebook. Kate O. (I'd known her sister, Nonnie) connected me with the 212 page. I began looking up people I remembered and sent out friend requests. I thought nobody would respond, but miraculously I became reacquainted with many of my former classmates.

The 50th reunion brought it all together. I surely wasn't incognito. People remembered me from my Facebook posts: the Chris Christie beach chair memes, the animal videos, the photos of my cat, Molly, and my many selfies. I met single women, mothers, and grandmothers whose lives were filled with fascinating careers, amazing accomplishments and beautiful families. I am so incredibly proud of each and every one of my sisters. I finally felt the sisterhood bond, and it was not an effort for me to fit in because I had found my way. We made plans to meet for lunch and to definitely keep in touch.

In 2020 the Covid-19 pandemic gripped our nation. Quarantines and face masks were the norm. There would be no lunches and keeping in touch was difficult, even with social media. Politics divided the country. There was no leadership. More importantly, Black men and women were being murdered. Americans marched and demonstrated to support the Black Lives Matter movement and to protest against racial injustices in law enforcement.

When we first began our Zoom sessions, it was such a relief to actually see people and hear their voices. In the beginning I was a bit apprehensive about sharing my personal life with many women that I had not seen since graduation. I felt comfortable with Facebook friends and those that I had met at the reunion, but others I did not remember at all. As the journey continued, many of my sisters became more open with their thoughts, opinions, and personal experiences. Some, like myself, just enjoyed listening to the others. I believe the camaraderie has deepened many friendships and made new ones.

The pandemic, with its many restrictions, has also given me a great deal of time to reflect on my life. The past seventy years have been a roller coaster ride, but through it all I have always tried to maintain a positive attitude, which I attribute to my quirky sense of humor. Although I worked in the accounting field for most of my life, it was never actually a career that I had dreamed of having. However, it paid the bills and gave me a certain degree of satisfaction. I do not have children, but I adore animals and have been blessed with eleven precious cats over the years. Molly, an adorable calico, has been my fur baby for ten years. She is the love of my life, and we are best friends. I enjoy my home, which I inherited from someone that I loved dearly. Every day I am surrounded by nature with all of its splendor. I have families of deer that often come to visit. Last spring, I actually witnessed the birth of a fawn which was quite an amazing experience. I am truly happy. As a free spirit, I am continuing to find my way as I enter a new chapter of a life that I believe has, thus far, been well lived.

Ambler, PA
November 2020

Karen Meketon Soskin

GHS 212 IN THE YEAR 2020

I'M WRITING ABOUT THE GHS 212 STORY I TOLD MYSELF and about seeing it differently in 2020. I apologize for unintentional missteps and for writing about the less familiar. I'm covering the less familiar because it has become important to me.

The backstory - the prequel – is a story many know. I went to the Philadelphia High School for Girls. I struggled. I wasn't smart enough. I finished every test thinking I flunked. I became addicted to this emotional model. I barely understood the concept of a boy. With one embarrassing exception, I wanted to be friends with everyone yet assumed nobody wanted to know me better beyond my circle. Eventually, I developed good study habits.

Race and diversity are part of the GHS backstory which I appreciate differently in 2021. I told myself I learned early: 1) the world is filled with smart women and 2) many smart women don't look like me. In classes, teachers called on me amid the Black girls, the Ukrainian girls, the South Philly girls. I learned stuff from a wide variety of girls in class. I was endlessly impressed with their intelligence.

The cafeteria merits mention. Sea of tables and chattering girls. I entered the cafeteria in dread of finding a seat among the Jewish girls. Where to put down my bookbag? Girls mingled in classes and then typically sat at homogenous lunch tables. At least, that was my impression. Two years ahead of me was my cousin, Janis Finkel. She ate with a circle of friends, class officers, popular girls. Sometimes, I'd stop by their table.

Their everyday constancy on lunch company contrasted with my furtive table searching.

I carried the story for 55 years that GHS was a great place to be for race and diversity.

Enter 2020. By now, I've lived by most major U.S. cities. I've sought - late in life - to make friends with black men and women. It has taken work, sensitivity, listening. (It hasn't been enough to talk about GHS.) My few black friends are accomplished – like my GHS classmates. I've come to recognize the key differentiator with those I know is socio-economic: in a phrase, my variety of friends all own cars (or live in Manhattan).

Since Black Lives Matter became familiar, it's seared into my brain that, being Jewish, there are people who don't see me as White. I am not White to white supremacists. One gigantic difference is that my complexion doesn't reveal who I am. If I sense I might be in a situation where someone might tell a Jewish joke, I make a pre-emptive strike to let it be known that I am Jewish.

I still work. I ended up with a dream job at 65: I work for a company dedicated to treating, preventing, curing HIV. When George Floyd was murdered, as part of a work team of 75, we got a grip on this fact: while we had recruited and onboarded diversely, equitable opportunity was not available. We were not doing right by all team members. Conversation circled me back to my GHS recollections. All mixed up in classes and cafeteria tables set so much by race, heritage, maybe AP classes. It's been similar in work settings. We go to the hotel bar lobby, and black colleagues tend to sit together at one end of the table. I've come to respect the support they give one another while mulling how I can't seem to give the same depth of support to them. Ongoing, I try to understand this more penetratingly.

How many conversations about race (in a company devoted to HIV patients yet) did it take for me to realize that white ones, at least sometimes, need to own the conversation about race and barriers inside our internal team?

I'm moving to GHS 212 Zoom calls. Probably, it was Theresa Jones Candis (who also saved a ticket for me for Anita Wise performing in Ambler the evening of our 50th reunion) who I remember speaking to the situation of being black at GHS. Thud onto my consciousness of another GHS dimension. The GHS 212 story I told myself for 55 years about race and diversity was never authenticated. I assembled it and liked the lullaby. It was a fairytale.

In addition to the thrill of GHS 212 faces and voices amid our common Covid reality, broadening my view for how else members of our class may have felt has been a window opened, an opportunity to remember more. I wonder if there are black friends to make now among my Zoom sisters.

Durham, NC
January 2021

Janice Miller Abrams

GOETHE, LEBOWITZ, AND ME *(OR IS IT I?)*

JANUARY 2021 - THE PANDEMIC IS SURGING. I HAVE SHEL-
tered in place, attended countless ZOOM lectures, discussions, meetings, and parties, and avoided the urge to redo all my closets. Now what?

The answer stares down at me. About 20 years ago in a fit of not-so-youthful exuberance, I wandered into a bookstore and purchased a copy of James Joyce's *Ulysses*. My frayed version from Dr. Goethe's class, with the mandatory Girls' High book cover, has long since vanished. I had gotten it into my head to re-read what I had so struggled with as a 17-year-old. Maybe having experienced a bit more of life I would connect as I had not before. Without grades or assignments or classes hanging over me, I thought I could fully engage. Unfortunately, this was not to be. There it sat, alongside other unread books, gathering dust but no creases for the better part of two decades – through four presidents, three moves, and a grandchild.

But now external distractions have evaporated. Time stretched. In nearly every conversation with friends, the topic of what we were reading came up in an interminably exhausting game of one-upmanship. It was the perfect time to drop a, "Well I thought it was a great opportunity to go back to *Ulysses*." This was the moment. And, let's face it, books are in! From CNN to TLC, every interviewer and interviewee has a well-appointed bookcase wedged between their head and the end of the screen. Like the Eiffel tower growing out of the skull of an enthusiastic tourist, the bookcase is ubiquitous. Would I climb my own mandatory backdrop and retrieve Ulysses? "Would I yes to say yes?"

Jane Murray Gilmore
B.Mus., M.Mus., M.Ed., D.M.A., Ed.D.

THE 212TH CLASS OF THE PHILADELPHIA HIGH SCHOOL FOR GIRLS

HAVING ALREADY BEEN ACCEPTED TO THE ONE ELE-mentary magnet school in Philadelphia, the Masterman School, I had hopes and dreams of attending the one elite magnet high school for gifted and academically talented girls, the Philadelphia High School for Girls. Nothing was taken for granted. I knew by attending this school, I would be fulfilling the dreams and aspirations of my mother, Alice Hodge Murray and her sister, my aunt, Edna Hodge Watkins, who had both attended Girls' High.

I prayed to God in earnest that I would pass the entrance test, be admitted and graduate. God answered my fervent prayers. I remained in prayer throughout my matriculation there.

When I attended Masterman, I went from being the smartest student in the class in my neighborhood elementary school to just one of the smart kids. There was an adjustment in workload and scholastic level, but my biggest adjustment was going from a school which was 99% African American to a school where I was a racial minority. Sometimes there were situations which I was not aware were racist until an adult brought it to my young, innocent eyes. By the time I reached the age of 13 and entered Girls' High, I was aware that racism existed.

Girls' High had its own challenges. It was like Masterman on steroids! The 212th class had 500 girls. Masterman had less than 500 students in the entire school. My first encounter with the school was "Freshman Orientation." Rules and staff members were introduced. My mom attended Girls' High when it was located in the Masterman School building. She beamed with pride to know that her daughter was one of the chosen. Out of the 500, there were less than 100 African American girls; I was a real minority here. Then the teachers came to the stage, each one older than the last. Finally, the physical education department teachers ascended to the stage. It looked like a geriatric ward! These are gym teachers? Then, my mom whispered, "She was my gym teacher for two years." What!!! There she was, a gym teacher walking with a cane! What could she possibly teach in gym? I eventually had her in 11th grade. The answer was "nothing" but beat the tom-tom when we did exercises. She always had one of the gymnasts or "Contest Girls" demonstrate how to do whatever.

Returning to orientation, we were divided alphabetically into groups to tour the school facilities. I was in section 410 (Miller-Orr). I knew one person, Shirley Miller, from church in my group, another who was in my 1st grade class, who probably did not remember me, and soon met Sandra Morgan. I realized how vast the facilities were with a field for outdoor activities, three main floors, a ground floor where the lunchroom and a few classrooms and offices were located, and basement, where the gyms were located. I discovered that if you had a class in the basement and your next class was on the third floor, you were allowed to use the elevator. That only happened in 10th grade when I had gym followed by Biology in room 302. All science classes were on the top floor. So, this was the beginning of high school at this prestigious school.

I soon discovered that the workload was tremendous, compared to nurturing Masterman, but not impossible. I curtailed several of my extracurricular activities to manage my workload. I stopped taking violin and clarinet because they were time consuming, yet I continued with piano lessons. I did not continue to Senior Girl Scouts; neither did any of my friends. Each teacher gave out assignments and scheduled tests as though their class was the only class. I quickly learned to take advantage of commuting time to do homework on the Broad Street Subway and the Market Street El, sometimes being so engrossed in the subject matter that I would ride past my stop and would have to cross over to ride back to the 52nd Street station.

My freshman roster consisted of:

ADVISORY - MISS O'NEIL, ROOM 217
My locker was right down the hall from that room.

ENGLISH - MISS L.
She frequently wore a particular suit that was green mohair. She had very keen features similar to a profile of a witch. In this class, I received my baptism by fire when I was first introduced to William Shakespeare's "A Midsummer Night's Dream." I was clueless as to what I was reading. Then I saw that some girls, who were answering most of the questions, had this thin yellow and black book. Puzzled, I sheepishly asked, "What's that?" They laughed and responded, "Cliff Notes! They help you under-stand these books better." I immediately went to a bookstore to buy these miracle notes. I immersed myself in reading the summaries and character descriptions. I finally could identify each character and his or her role. I then knew who Puck was and what was supposed to be experienced by read-ing the play. I drenched myself with reading and memorizing excerpts of Shakespearean works from freshman through senior year of high school. Thank you, Cliff Notes, for helping me through 12 Shakespearean works and the other literature. In 9th grade, the entire class read "The Odyssey" and Edith Hamilton's "Mythology." It was a rough year in English. I had to get used to reading 50 pages per night of difficult, antiquated, boring

literature. Even writing compositions was not a safe haven. I soon discovered my essay writing, which usually received B+ or better in middle school, was no longer acceptable at Girls' High, no indeed not! I wrote and wrote. Then the graded paper would be returned with soooo many "red marks" with soooo many corrections. I remember setting up appointments to talk with the teacher, redoing assignments, asking for suggestions, etc. The red marks became less and less. Towards the end of the year, she wrote, "You have become a writer. Good job!" I was shocked, yet appreciative of all the scrutiny she had done. What a year!

GEOMETRY - ROOM 313

I passed the Algebra I test and was placed in geometry with Mr. S. I couldn't find that new room after getting my roster changed and ended up missing a week of classes. I was completely lost by that time. He had no sympathy for the fact that I was a freshman who was placed in his class late. When I told him that I needed help, his response was that he would have to start from the beginning, and he was not willing to do that. He said, "Take it next year when you are a sophomore!" He wore coke bottle glasses. When he wrote on the board, his head was almost touching it. In the sunlight one could see the chalk dust flying as he wrote. He was a true mathematician, brilliant and inflexible.

Thank goodness for a student who belonged to my church who helped me. I was completely lost in geometry. I had never, ever come that close to failing a class. I tried getting an after-school tutor, but to no avail. I was embarrassed because I had never had to ask for help. At my church there was a young Central graduate, who was then in college, majoring in math, who started tutoring me, but to no avail. Then another older student at my church heard of my plight. Tutoring arrangements were made between my mother and her. Linda was a senior at West Philadelphia High School. She felt that tutoring me would help her to review for the SAT's.

Linda was very candid with me, telling me that I needed to start from the very beginning and would probably fail several other tests until I actually caught up with my class. She was RIGHT! She tutored me every Saturday from 10 am to 5 pm for several weeks until I caught up to my class, then I was a force to be reckoned with. I started getting A's. The teacher made me take a retest after school because he thought that I had cheated. My grade was even higher. I went from an "F" average for the first marking period to a final grade of "B". I received an award for the most improved math student. That was my most challenging time at Girls' High. I regained my confidence in math.

WORLD HISTORY - MRS. C.

She was OK. She taught a lot of information. We had to read and outline chapters EVERY night for homework. I did well because I was good at regurgitating facts and memorizing dates for all those essays at the end of all those fill in the blank questions without clues. There were never multiple-choice tests. That would be too easy! It might jar your memory. No, never! Just know those cold hard facts! I did well here!

FRENCH I

This was my first experience in learning a foreign language other than the snippets of Latin and learning the difference between English words in the UK and the United States. I was excited but did not know what to expect. I discovered that I enjoyed it! It was refreshing to have a subject that was new to everyone; we were all at the same level. My teacher was Madame Waldbaum. She was a pleasant, patient, knowledgeable teacher who made learning fun. Classes were enjoyable. I felt that I had now gained new, valuable life skills of reading, speaking and listening in a foreign language.

GYM

I had one of those old teachers! It was fun. We did a variety of activities. In the fall, there was field hockey. Later we played baseball, soccer and basketball, climbed ropes, jumped stationary horses, tumbled on mats, swung on rings, did floor dances, etc. All to complete various goals to receive a grade for each skill. It was a true learning experience.

MUSIC ELECTIVES

1. Treble Clef - Mr. Murphy
    Rehearsals were before school in Room 205, three times a week. Very few freshmen were privileged enough to be selected to be in Treble Clef, the school choir, but I had been recommended by Virginia Hagemann, the music teacher at Masterman. I loved music and Mr. Murphy.

2. I had an after-school organ class for pianists twice a week with Mrs. June Hires. At the end of the school year, I was chosen to play the "Academic Festival Overture Finale" on the organ for the National Catholic Music Teachers Convention, which was being held in Philadelphia that year. That was my first time performing in public on the organ. From that experience I and several others were given stipends to begin organ lessons at Settlement Music School, thus resulting in our future music careers.

These were the pleasurable classes at GHS.

I have no intention of going through each class that I had at GHS, but a few stand out for various reasons:

10TH GRADE - FOREIGN LANGUAGES, FRENCH II - MISS ROTH

Wow, Girls' High has a young teacher! Her hair was BLACK, not gray! She spoke quietly in French and English. I liked French simply because it was refreshing to continue learning a foreign language with a young teacher!

I had done so well in French I, I was permitted to take a 5th major. I chose to begin Spanish I. I had Miss Adinolfi for all three years. It was an instant "A."

10TH GRADE – ENGLISH - DR. FAUST

She talked to her plants which were growing so beautifully on the windowsills. The most memorable pieces of literature were "A Tale of Two Cities" by Charles Dickens and Shakespeare's "Julius Caesar." I still remember that we were seated in alphabetical order according to our last names. We were assigned to memorize Marc Antony's famous speech:

> "Friends, Romans, countrymen, lend me your ears;
> I come to bury Caesar, not to praise him.
> The evil that men do lives after them;
> The good is oft interred with their bones;
> So let it be with Caesar...."

This leads me to:

10TH GRADE BIOLOGY!!!

I was placed in a star biology class. At one point in my life, I had thought about becoming a physician. This one experience in biology class at Girls' High caused me to change my career path completely because I never, ever wanted to be under as much psychological stress as I encountered that year. The teacher, Ms. G, was my first African American teacher at GHS, but very difficult. She was new to Girls' High. She often mentioned that she was a graduate of the other GHS, Germantown High School, since Girls' High did not accept her. This biology class was extremely demanding, and we were often taught from the teacher's medical books (she had been in medical school at some point). She even deducted points for spelling errors.

On this particular day, we had received our report cards. Most of us, although we had worked tirelessly, were disappointed in our grade in biology. Several classmates and I had tried to get out of the class, but to no avail. Many students had failed in this teacher's class. The girls in my class were supposed to have been the better students, yet our failure rate was dismal. I was just thankful that I passed with a "D." One of the brightest girls in the

GIRLS HIGH SCHOOL, A SCHOOL WITH MANY TRADITIONS

SCHOOLWIDE

1. Your friends made bows of candy and goodies for you to wear and nibble on your birthday. All day long, you were wished Happy Birthday.

2. Decorated lockers

3. County Fair

4. Assemblies with the school orchestra playing as you entered

5. Class meetings in the gym

6. Campaigning and elections of class officers in the gym

7. Bell schedules

8. Winter Shows (Treble Clef Candlelight Procession on "Hodie" and singing all of or excerpts from Benjamin Britten's "A Ceremony of Carols")

9. Spring Shows

10. Songs of the season in different languages

11. Treble Clef Caroling

12. All the shows and special assemblies

13. Contest

FRESHMAN TRADITION

1. 9th grade picnic at Burholme Park (I had no idea where I was in the city).

SOPHOMORE SPECIAL EVENTS

1.   10th grade trip to the Shakespeare Theater in Stratford, CT, a 1,500-seat venue modeled after the Globe Theatre in London. It was the home of the American Shakespeare Festival. The Connecticut theater burned down in 2019.

2.   10th Grade Dance: I couldn't go because my parents thought that I was too young, having been skipped a grade in school.

JUNIOR YEAR NICETIES

1.   11th grade Tea

2.   Contest participation (I'm not athletic, but I marveled at those who were).

3.   Junior Promenade (Prom)
     I double dated with my best friend, Carolynn Hayward. Our dates knew each other, too, which made it fun. A house load of friends and relatives saw us off. I was finally allowed to go on a real live date.

THE EXCITEMENT OF MY SENIOR YEAR!

At last! I was a senior at Girls' High. The preparation began before I stepped into the building to take my rightful position as a senior. During the summer, I had an appointment to go to the photography studio to have my graduation pictures taken, one with a shoulder drape and the other with a sweater. I must admit that they were the most beautiful pictures that I ever had taken in my life. I hardly recognized myself. I no longer looked like that frightened girl who had walked through those doors years before as a freshman. I was beginning to look like a young woman, ready to face the world.

After being out of school for summer vacation for a few days, I became bored because many of my friends had to go to summer school for review courses, so I had nobody to talk to during the day. I enrolled in summer school to take an advanced course in an AP class called "Political Science and American Government," supposedly to lighten my load. I had to get permission from my counselor. Mrs. Carson was still at the school cleaning her office, so I was able to get the sought-after approval. The course was EXCELLENT! It was so engaging and taught me information on civics which I carry with me until this day. The class culminated with several trips; one to Harrisburg to view our state government and a trip to Capitol Hill to experience the workings of our federal government in Washington, DC. My class of eleven was able to meet both state and federal officials.

I entered my senior year with the fervor and determination to make this year "The Best." However, my roster was not what I thought it was going to be. I had always had five majors since sophomore year, therefore, I thought it was time to relax. I thought that I would have English IV, Spanish III, drop French IV, Calculus, no Social Science since I took the summer AP course, no Science because I had already fulfilled my requirements, Treble Clef and PE/HE. My counselor, whom I thought was my friend, had filled in classes. My roster read as: English IV*, Spanish III*, French IV*, Calculus, Physics and Treble Clef with a PE contract. The "star" classes were Advanced Placement or AP classes. I protested but the counselor called my mother to tell her that I was eligible to take these classes. In addition, it was lonely being in star classes. In some classes I was the only Black student. The other students stayed with their friends. I hated working in groups because most of the time I had to ask to join unless the observant teachers assigned students to groups. Then I knew that once the assignment ended, it would be business as usual. I really did not like to be singled out or the one token. Friends were important to me. That year, particularly, I wanted to reinforce those friendships that I had established in earlier years so that I would leave GHS with lifetime friendships. In other words, I wanted to have a life other than going to school, practice and studying. I felt comfortable about my chances of getting into a "good" college, so what was the rationale for punishing myself this year? By taking these courses, I would increase my class rank. I did get out of the English IV* after pleading with my mom and the counselor. I knew English classes at GHS could be grueling. They could make you stay up all night to read and interpret literature and to write term papers. I convinced them that I would have so much additional work preparing college applications, studying for the SAT's and practicing organ and piano in order to prepare for auditions for college that it would not be beneficial. Thank God, they finally listened. I made honor roll, but it was more challenging than what I had anticipated.

I enjoyed all the activities of my senior year. Besides the school wide activities, which I mentioned previously, there were:

1. Getting your best friend to write your personal description for the yearbook.

2. Senior Class Trip - Washington, DC by train

3. Senior Days at School

4. Contest

   I admired all of my classmates who participated in Contest. They were quite impressive. I remember our mascot was "Peter Pan." The opposing team's mascot was "Siegfried."

   As the excitement was building in the Girls' High gym, our nation was experiencing a tragedy. The foremost civil rights leader of our time, the Rev. Dr. Martin Luther King, Jr., was assassinated on April 6, 1968 in Memphis, Tennessee. My thoughts were of uncontrollable grief. Here was our strong, much revered Black leader who fought for equal justice for all, especially for Blacks. He was the peaceful warrior. He fought by using nonviolent tactics, yet he was killed violently. What is wrong with the U.S., a place where we are not judged by our merits but by the color of the skin that God gave us when He created us? I thought of all the many times when I was dis-criminated against in school. I wondered if all of my hard work at Girls' High would make a difference. Would my life have been easier, different or better if I had been born white? These were some of the thought-provoking questions which occurred during this period. I experienced sadness and grief but also anger. I had been told all of my life by parents, teachers, family and friends of family that I had to be not just good, but excellent because of my race. Now I realized that excellence sometimes gets you killed. Now what?

Some of the happy excitement was taken from Contest after this tragic event. The teams played. Finally, Contest was over! The score was being tabulated. Dr. Ruth Murray Klein, our principal, appeared with hats from both the 212th and 213th classes. We waited with great anticipation. She raised both hats indicating it was a tie! Another disappointment of our senior year!

5. Senior Class Play (I had a part to sing, "Cold Popsicles, Cold," but I took myself out because I thought that my voice sounded too operatic).

6. Senior Prom

I had looked forward to the elegance and pageantry of my Senior Prom. Everything had to be perfect! I chose my friend, Michael David Gilmore, as my date. I had attended his Senior Prom almost two years prior. He was a graduate of Overbrook High School. I had met him when we were both students at Masterman, but then we were not considered friends. After several years had transpired, we were set up as a blind date for his Senior Prom, and the rest is history. We dated several times by going to dinner, movies and bowling. We sometimes double-dated with his older brother and his date.

That previous September Mike matriculated as a freshman scholarship student at Howard University in Washington, DC. Once he was in college, he wrote to me EVERY week. We would go on dates on the weekends when he came home. Then he started to go to church with me and later joined my church.

That evening, he was a flawless diamond, satisfying all my requirements: intelligent, polite, respectful, a sense of humor, nice smile, handsome, a perfect gentleman. I was proud to have him as my date. I thoroughly enjoyed being with Mike and my girlfriends with their dates at both the prom at the City Line Marriott and the breakfast at the Shelron Ballroom in Cheltenham. It was all that I had envisioned and more. It was an evening of complete elegance, surpassing all of my dreams. Four years later, after my graduation from Boston University, Mike became my wonderful husband.

7. Vietnam War

    In talking to some of my classmates at the Prom, I noticed a few of them were somewhat melancholy. I discovered that some of their original Prom dates could not attend because they had been either drafted, injured or killed in the Vietnam War. It made one realize that there was a war going on that only impacted my classmates and me minimally since we were attending an all-female academic school. I later realized that the ramifications of the war on all-male and coed schools with a high rate of male dropouts or males not attending college, was devastating. This realization was a foreshadowing of my college years in Boston, when I saw on campus the anti-war demonstrations, burning of draft cards, sit-ins, civil rights demonstrations, etc. The Vietnam War was what I experienced only when I viewed it on television. At this stage of my life, I knew nobody who had gone to Vietnam to fight. By attending the Philadelphia High School for Girls, I had lived a very sheltered life.

8. Graduation

    It was June! It was our last month attending our soon to be Alma Mater. Nothing could go wrong being so close to the end. The 212th class of GHS was smaller than it was in our freshman and sophomore years. I could tell by my section number. In 9th grade and 10th, I was in sections 410 and 311, respectively. In 11th grade I was in section 210 and in my senior year, 109. So many of the Black girls that I had befriended were returned to their neighborhood schools. (A few I met later in adulthood; some were successful, and others were not.) They were all traumatized by the Girls' High experience. There were no support systems in place to help them to be successful. I had just discovered in a conversation with one of my best Jewish friends that some of the Jewish teachers tutored the Jewish students during the summer so that they could be successful the next year. Wow, that was a game changer! My success was without that added staff support and I still did relatively well.

We started "Count Down to Zero Day"- Graduation (no classes, just rehearsals). At each lunch period, one could hear the thunderous banging on the lunchroom tables declaring the number of days when all classes would end for us forever at Girls' High! On Zero Day, we wore a doughnut, a bagel or an "0" around our necks. What could ever happen to take away our joy? Then tragedy struck again! Presidential candidate Robert F. Kennedy, a younger brother of the assassinated president, John F. Kennedy, was himself assassinated in Los Angeles after a campaign stop. Again?

This was awful! Another assassination of a prominent figure within months AND the second assassination experienced by the same family as another of its sons was again gunned down. I concluded at this early age that something was seriously wrong with our country and its values. My prayer to God was that I would safely graduate from high school without encountering any of this violence.

Finally, graduation day was upon us. My mom had taken me downtown to get my beautiful white dress and shoes needed for graduation. This would be my first graduation. I did not graduate from elementary or middle schools because Masterman went up to 9th grade. I left there at the end of 8th grade, thus missing all the graduation rituals of lower grades including autograph books.

My graduation day was wonderful! I was somewhat disappointed that the ceremony was not held at the beautiful Academy of Music because of renovations, but rather at the Civic Center near Convention Hall. The ceremony was wonderful as each girl, dressed in white and carrying long-stemmed, red roses, proudly knew, "We had survived!" I thank God for the day which not only fulfilled my dreams but the hopes and dreams of my mother and my aunt, both of whom had attended Girls' High, and my late grandmother. My grandmother had graduated from Shaw University in Raleigh, NC, passed the Philadelphia teachers' test and was issued a train ticket to come to Philadelphia to teach high school English at the end of the 19th century. Needless to say, she was denied the opportunity when it was discovered that she was Black. Her accommodations were denied. She had to stay in a Black rooming house. Later they offered her a position to teach the dock workers how to read and write. There she met my grandfather who was a foreman since he had some literacy. This graduation meant much more than anyone could have ever imagined! Off to college in the Fall, the first in my family to do so in two generations. Girls' High had over-prepared me academically. I now know the meaning of the GHS motto, "Vincit qui se vincit," guiding me throughout life. Thank you, Girls' High!

Laverock, PA
February 2021

Fran Nachman

MAKING LEMONADE
FROM LEMONS

WHAT A YEAR! 2020 WILL BE ONE FOR THE RECORD books. The tragic loss of lives. The not knowing when this will end and the subsequent impact to our mental and emotional well-being. The fear of catching COVID-19. So many people continue to struggle financially to meet basic needs for themselves and their families.

But there also have been silver linings. Since early spring we have seen an outpouring of kindness demonstrated by people across the world. In the spring we watched inspiring videos of New Yorkers, as well as Europeans, on their balconies each night banging pots and pans, playing music and singing, to honor the selfless healthcare workers that risked their own health, as well as the health of their families, to treat COVID patients. And the generosity of people donating their time and money to assist those in need often brought tears to my eyes.

The environment has benefited, at least in the short term. With reduced consumption of gas and oil, pollution has decreased, and oceans are clearer for the first time in decades. In San Francisco, sparrows have changed their tune. In the past they competed with urban noise, causing their mating calls to be loud and shrill. As more people remained home, they lowered their voices, and their songs became more "sultry."

We are connecting and reconnecting with friends and family, realizing it is human interaction that will help to keep us sane in this surreal world, and provide us with emotional nourishment. This year we discovered if we are not able to connect in person there are other ways to "see" each other. Each week I FaceTime with one of my best friends, a Brooklyn native who still resides there. Gail and I met the summer after our high school graduations as apprentices at Forestburgh Summer Theater in the Catskills. As I was someone who had visions of becoming an actress, Jane Cotner, my history teacher and head of the drama department, referred me to this program. Gail and I were roommates that summer and have remained friends since. Our annual vacation to Rehoboth, where we traveled with our sons from the time they were four and six, until they "aged out", was sadly cancelled this year for the first time in over twenty years.

Since March, there have been an endless stream of podcasts and webinars. Some were professional or educational, while others were purely social. And a few, like my book club (and our Girls' High Zoom meetings), were a combination. As a hotel concierge since 2007, my beloved profession (my third career after seven years in film production and owning a business for 25+ years), was in jeopardy, as concierge desks throughout the world were closing. Every month I attended webinars from Forbes Travel and Les Clefs d'Or (the international association of hotel concierges of which I'm proud to be a member.) They were informative, and provided a sense of community, acknowledging that many of us were facing the same emotional challenges regarding our work situation. Even during the darkest days, I remain hopeful that the hospitality industry will make a successful comeback by next summer and I will return to work.

Merriam-Webster recently named "pandemic" as the word of the year, but I'm sure that Zoom could have been one of the finalists. From neophyte grandparents to IT pros, we all (or at least most of us) learned how to mute and switch to gallery view. I am so grateful to our classmates who organized and hosted our Zoom meetings. What a terrific way to "see" friends and acquaintances from 50+ years ago (I find it really painful to type that number!) It's been great to catch up on each other's lives, whether still living in the Philly area, or somewhere across the US and even Europe. We were even able to watch from Candy Whitman's Barcelona balcony as her neighbors banged pots and pans to honor their local healthcare workers.

How shocked I was to discover how many of my classmates did not have an ideal experience during their Girls' High years. While I always had one or two best friends, I never felt I belonged to the "popular" crowd. I attributed some of this to the decision I made to remain at Leeds Jr. High for 9th grade, believing that it would be more fun to be the "big girl on campus" rather than the lowly freshman. While I never regretted that decision, (9th grade was my favorite year at school) I did feel it put me at a disadvantage as I felt that many GHS friendships were formed that first year.

Over the years I attended several reunions. All were wonderful experiences of sharing memories. We are such an amazing group of accomplished women, either currently working, or retired from so many diverse careers. We were so fortunate to attend Girls' High, where we were all expected to attend college and lead successful lives, both at home and at work This was not the norm for female high school students in 1968. I particularly loved when we separated into "neighborhood" groups and took pictures with classmates that we knew as young children. While this is typical at most high schools, both Girls' High and Central drew their student bodies from across the city.

It was during these Zoom meetings that tough topics were raised, and some of us recalled their painful high school experiences. As a 17-year-old at graduation, I look back and realize how ill-equipped we were to handle the emotional ups and downs that come with being a teenager. This makes me more empathetic to young people today, who face even more challenging issues caused by social media. Zoom calls were also a sad reminder of who I was not able to "see." Andrea Rose (Panofsky) was my best friend in high school. We went to prom together (triple dating with Lily Samuel (Rothman). Andrea married Alan, her date that night, and they had two children that I still stay in contact with. We were supposed to grow old together, but she died nearly thirty years ago. Although Rita Freedman and I were not friends in high school, we became close when studying for our MBA's, and travel "buddies" for several years, touring Scandinavia, Switzerland and Italy, as well as our last trip to Colorado and Utah. Rita also lost her battle with breast cancer and died almost ten years ago. I planned to attend the wedding of her daughter Mimi, a physician in Seattle, scheduled for September. But it has been postponed until next spring. My own May wedding in Phoenix is now planned for next June.

For many years I strongly believed the expression that "when one door closes, another opens." Time and time again, experience has shown me that when a negative situation arises, there will be a more positive one on the horizon. For me, this year has been about making pitchers of lemonade from lemons. I have so much to feel grateful for. Everyone in my family is healthy. I'm at the fittest I've been since my 20's, both my fiancé and my son have successful careers, and I'm fortunate to have wonderful friends. There is positive news about two or more successful vaccine trials. And Joe Biden is our President-Elect!! As I said, there is so much for which to be grateful.

Philadelphia, PA
December 2020
fgn2479@gmail.com

Linda Notto Stulz

AND THEN I WAS SAVED

WHEN WE WERE IN EIGHTH GRADE OUR ELEMENTARY school arranged a school bus trip to the local Catholic High School for academic placement testing. Entering in line, we were yelled at for it not being straight enough. We were yelled at for not putting our name cards in correct alphabetical order. I think we misplaced the Mc name. We were told we were not worthy of attending that school.

In the meantime, a neighbor's older sister was attending the University of Pennsylvania, having been one of the top five students in her high school class. She advised our mothers to consider Girls' High because her peers at Penn who had attended Girls' High were well adjusted in the college classroom while she found the teaching style at Penn challenging.

We each secured an appointment for yet another placement test, rode the subway thirty minutes, and emerged at the school on a hill. At my appointment, I was met by a gracious "sister" who welcomed me and gave a tour of the school. The counselor shook my hand. The classroom had no crucifix. A deep breath later, I committed to being on my own... When my mother asked how it went; I replied, "No contest, I'm going to Girls' High!" The pastor called her to dissuade her from allowing this. She was president of the PTA, a church volunteer, a political volunteer, and a judge of elections. She was a neighborhood force. She stood firm, supporting my decision. I wonder if she knew how much she was appreciated. One could end here and state "the rest is history". But it was just the beginning.

Those thirty minutes on the subway each day? Coming from the source stop a few blocks south, the cars were sparsely populated in the morning, so the few people you saw became the same each day. We smiled, sat next to each other, chatted, then began to wait on the platform for each other and board the same car. Down in that dirty tunnel, I met the girls who became my dearest, cherished lifelong friends.

The education was more, much more than academic, although that was brain expanding. The girls were from every part of the city and were every ethnicity. In my neighborhood people were White or Black, mostly Italian, all Catholic. At Girls' High I met Ukrainian, Lithuanian, Amish, Asian, Irish, and Italian girls; and they were not Catholic. They were Jewish, Baptist, and atheist for all I knew. The constrictions no longer applied.

Then there were the teachers: Dr. Faust, the first person I ever heard who questioned the government's use of her taxes. Mrs. Rubinstein, who encouraged us to have fun because we studied too much! The science teacher who told us to not just be good, "Be Good at Something". The music teacher who played the Beatles to classroom snickers and told us not to be music snobs. The geometry teacher who encouraged us by saying that we might design a city subway system someday. The history teacher who introduced me to the 'New York Times' and 'The Wall Street Journal'. The Philosophy Club, The Folksong Society. The Civil Rights movement. ON and ON...

Then we went on to college, careers (some illustrious), families, tragedies, heartbreak and joy. We sometimes lost touch in the demands of life. If we were fortunate enough to travel, we met sisters along the way and enriched our lives further. Then, as is obvious now, our lives slowed dramatically. Quarantined, cautious about the most common activities. Some people used creativity to maintain connections beyond their mask while others discovered that their personal cocoon was enough. Perhaps a curious person, a Girls' High girl, will study this phenomenon? I hope so. But this group of 212 women reached out and suggested we utilize technology to connect and reconnect. Interacting with women not seen for many years resulted in long and fruitful conversations of contrasting life arcs. Funny, painful, honest.

At each Zoom meeting, I appreciated the discussions, purchased the book recommendations, viewed the films, and was overall inspired by the group. Then Margit and Susan suggested we contribute to a group writing project! Oh no, they have gone too far! But upon reflection, I am thankful for the opportunity to put down some thoughts about our place in this time, our place as young girls, and the memories that connect us.

Thank a virus? Thank some fellow travelers through this life.

A COVID HAIKU

A lifetime journey
A new virus interrupts
My friends sustain me.

Maple Glen, PA
December 2020

There were girls in my class who were good in math and science. I was not one of them. I always thought they were smarter than me because, after all, they easily understood what was a struggle for me. It's odd, how we don't value talents that are natural, and yearn instead for what is hard.

I'd like to tell you that French remained an important part of my life, but it didn't. After majoring in French in college and being accepted in French PhD programs, I abruptly gave it up and pursued a different career. Being passionate is part of being young, and changing passions is too.

Fast forward fifty years: thanks to Covid here I am together again with girls I went to school with, now accomplished women. It's clear that much of what we thought important then means nothing to us now. We've grown up, matured, evolved. Yet, in some ways we are the same. If you want to see real passion, ask a group of Girls' High girls how they feel about one space (versus two) between sentences. Maybe we are not as different as I thought. I love my GHS classmates for the amazing women they have become, and I love them for the Girls' High girls they will always be.

Havertown,PA
January 2021
www.margitnovack.com

Sharon Ozlek Dunoff shares a big welcoming hug from Candace Whitman on her visit to Candace's apartment in Barcelona in December 2017

Sharon Ozlek Dunoff

NOT QUITE ALWAYS
THE PROCRASTINATOR

MY 2010'S, WITH A FEW EXCEPTIONS FOR LOVELY vacations, sucked. The decade began with the end of a forty-year friend- ship, then a bout with cancer ("the good kind", Hodgkin's Lymphoma) in 2012, which I believe developed from the stress of losing that precious relationship. Major mental health issues erupted in the family in 2014, followed by the death of a close friend from cancer in 2015 and that of our beloved family matriarch at just short of age 88 in 2016. More mental health crises occurred in 2018, and my closest work buddy retired to Florida in 2019. I anticipated a brand-new decade with a mixture of dread and hope for less trauma. Thanks to therapy and medication, I rarely look back, believing that the future has to be better than the past. (One exception: I peaked in academic achievement in 11th and 12th grade at GHS, somehow graduating 6th in our class, by working hard, nose to the grindstone, but always cramming to meet deadlines up to the last minute! Never managed to match that standing at Penn.)

But, I digress. When the pandemic hit, I panicked. My lifestyle, even after age sixty was always full of social outings, classes, concerts, and reasons to get out of the house, avoiding the clutter that lived there. Not the hoarded kind of piles that don't allow people to cross the room, but enough to get on my husband's nerves because it flowed into the family room of our open floor plan living space, as well as our bedroom and my "office" upstairs. Again, my procrastinating nature pushed back and it took most of 2020 before I got myself in gear enough to allow the replacement of our thirty-year-old wall to wall carpeting on the second floor and a "new" set of used office furniture to move into my room. After unloading overflowing bookcases, books and papers are still under scrutiny from the basement to the second floor as far as where they will reside or whether I can part with them. But progress is being made.

The push that moved me toward accepting the restrictions of living under the pandemic and facing the inevitable truth that there was no better time to take on the overwhelming task of decluttering and organizing my stuff came from an unusual source: my introduction to the IJS Daily Sit, Monday to Friday at 12:30 pm. My dear friend since age seven, Meryl, told me about the Institute for Jewish Spirituality which offers this free weekday wonder through Zoom. Hosted by rabbis and cantors worldwide, who mix commentary on Torah with Buddhist meditation, the poetry of Rumi, and other inspiring elements, followers are guided through the practice of mindfulness in a beautifully accessible way that I believe people of all religions can appreciate.

I can't explain exactly how the mindfulness meditation practice helped me reduce procrastination. Perhaps it interrupted the tendency toward perfectionism that sometimes stops one from doing something challenging and encouraged self-compassion, a quality that those of us who weathered our competitive upbringing can certainly use more of, regardless of how conventionally "successful" we are. I am so grateful to Meryl for sharing this resource with me which has had a profound effect on my daily life.

In addition to the spiritual practice I adopted in 2020, I stepped up to work on the political campaigns that I couldn't in good conscience ignore. Many hours of phone banking and in person canvassing (masked and physically distanced from front doors, of course) made a tiny but rewarding contribution to the election of Joe Biden. As our young team organizer reminded us, "You don't want to wake up on November 6th with Trump reelected, berating yourself for not making that extra call." I met some incredibly dedicated volunteers, as well as paid staff, who put forth tireless effort to win the election, not taking anything for granted while following strict guidelines to protect everyone from Covid. I was proud to be a part of that effort and was surprised to receive a couple of presents from friends who wanted to acknowledge what I did. That was a great feeling! But, given the events of January 6, 2021, we can't rest on our laurels.

There is more work to do, internally as well as externally. As I'm currently reading *How to Be an Anti-Racist*, I struggle with how to make my interactions in the 2020's, including those on Zoom, more inclusive than those of the past decade, which primarily focused on coping with personal trauma. In addition to speaking out to lessen the stigma and fund the treatment of mental illness across the population, I'm hoping to find more areas of common interest with people of color that can bring us together. Maybe that will be on the political scene again... but maybe there are other paths as yet undiscovered. As we approach seventy, however, there is no more time to procrastinate!

Havertown, PA
February 2021

Jane Pearl Barr

MY 2020:
A YEAR IN REVIEW

PROLOGUE: CONTEXT FOR MY STORIED STRUGGLE. I would love to be a writer; I dread writing. While I majored in English in college, my graduate studies embraced psychology and law. I perseverated as if dictated clinical diagnostic and treatment notes should be publishable. I do not publish legal decisions.

I was the last judge sitting in family court in Manhattan on March 25. Why? Because I didn't say no. I was exposed to Covid-19, and experienced symptoms 13 days later. It was too frightening to go to the hospital for testing because that is where people were dying. My doctor big brother saved my life by telling me in April to do everything he had researched which might help, and I followed his guidance, chapter and verse. I recovered to learn I had no antibodies. What? But emergency room nurses who have tested positive for the virus also have tested negative for antibodies.

My roof, which is the footprint of our Manhattan two bedroom apartment in Murray Hill, saved me, physically and spiritually, during Spring, 2020. I literally would crawl up the spiral staircase in our kitchen to a lounge chair ensconced in heavy towels to worship the vitality of sun and fresh air, and plants and birds, all of which were enhanced immeasurably by the shut down of New York City and, therein, far far fewer emissions. The crowning smile of each day came from the resounding clapping and cheering and horns, and sometimes musical instruments and shouts, celebrating our first responders.

I reimagined daily exercise at home with aerobic and Jane Fonda and Qigong videos, and this truly worked, nicely subbing for the gym and Pilates at 6:30 AM. I also learned to work hard at home, doing cases virtually, some days and weeks for as many hours as when I physically had sat in court. Working helped me to look beyond myself, and required my learning new technological skills. A highlight was having a grand-dog, and witnessing my daughter and son-in-law nurture their puppy. A lowest light was the frightening understandable violence which erupted across our country, with ensuing sounds of helicopters and sights of boarded up windows everywhere. What would follow the Corona virus and viral violence?

For me what followed was having a CT scan on July 2nd, receiving a diagnosis on July 7th of Stage 1A lung cancer, and undergoing laparoscopic surgery on July 13th; no lymph node involvement, no surrounding tissue encroachment and, thus, no radiation, chemotherapy, or preventive immunotherapy - rather, CT scans to be scheduled every three months for whatever number of years. As cancer goes, I was lucky. My cloud's platinum lining was spending hospital time with my daughter before and after on the day of surgery - the first time we spent significant time together (other than our dogs' play dates and quick distanced dinners on our roof) since we took a weekend spa getaway just before the pandemic marathon. I also relished tasting Sen Chan Pad Lobster Noodle delivered by my son-in-law in lieu of hospital cuisine.

Between CT and surgery, however, for the first time in my life I experienced an abrupt pause to my integral looking forward to the future. I felt adhered to a murky present, devoid of my Manhattan frenetic poster-child cultural diversions, hovering on a frightening precipice of imminent fixed focus on the past. No.

I needed something bigger than myself, bigger than my day job, bigger than my professional and personal board director positions. I needed the profound hope of a next chapter. I found this hope in my most cherished combination of travel and work.

I spent my summer working, recovering, and preparing my Fulbright U.S. Scholarship Professional Project Application for the Maldives, to work in juvenile justice and, hopefully, also child protection and family violence prevention. My application was completed before the September 15th deadline.

My autumn's highlight was spending Thanksgiving with our daughter and son-in-law in Croton-on-Hudson. We all tested negative before the holiday, were given printed menus and plated food, and sat at safely spaced tables able to see each other, with windows and front door open - the food was gourmet, delicious, and thoughtfully accommodating of my gluten-free and my husband's meatless and dairy-free dietary restrictions; the wine was divine; and the company of our son-in-law's immediate family was spectacular.

I always felt uncomfortable, beginning in childhood, with the inexplicably hypocritical context of Thanksgiving. I suffered in silence what was awry for me, and was absolutely fine if not relieved when, on occasion, I didn't feel well and missed one or two Thanksgiving celebrations throughout the years. This year, I simply enjoyed my best Thanksgiving ever!

On December 21st, my winter solstice was marked by my learning that my Fulbright Application had been approved to pass on to the host country for review and consideration. The email was clear - no guarantee, don't make plans, wait. I understand. It feels quite nice that the Fulbright U.S. Scholar Program has deemed me good enough to pass on to the Maldives, for their consideration. Que sera sera.

New York, NY
February 2021

Many of us discovered we dated as far back as elementary school…

Eileen Perkins Lashin's kindergarten photo dated 1955 Pennell Elementary. She's seated in chair first row, bottom right. Arlene Margolis Slepchik is also in the class, 2nd row from the top, 4th from the right. Can you find Eileen's twin, Renee or Arlene Suttin Roman? Anyone else you recognize?

AB Day School 1956. Identifiable are Denise Morrison Stroller, Sharon Greenspan, Nancy Snyder Wallace and Susan Dukow. Can you find them, yourself or name any others?

Eileen Perkins Lashin

DECEMBER 2020

It's hard to believe that I will be reaching that 70-year-old milestone this December 25th. I am grateful to be here, to be healthy, and to have "more than enough" time to myself. Yes, I am happily married for 44 years and my spouse and I are very devoted to one another. However, I love my friends and treasure my bonds and connections with them. I also relish reconnecting with friends, colleagues, fellow classmates, acquaintances, etc.

These pandemic months have been a time of isolation yet I do not feel all alone, as I reach out to others by phone, email, FaceTime, etc. But I miss the human connection! I have been able to get together with friends outdoors for walks and talks and we have been fortunate to visit our children on a limited and planned basis. Nothing is spontaneous.

It took some time for me to find my niche after I retired 4 years ago. I worked as an administrator for a non-profit child care program. I loved my job, but was ready to shift gears. Within a few years, we went from 0 to 4 grandchildren, now ages 5 and under. They are the "bright lights" in my life and I adore them. In addition to nurturing my grandchildren, I also felt a strong need to cultivate new connections. I started to volunteer for a few programs and enjoyed being involved this way. Only one program now is operational due to the pandemic and it is all virtual. I love participating in this program, Safe Harbor. The program provides grief counseling and support to children and adolescents who sadly have suffered the loss of a parent, sibling, close friend, etc. I meet with a group of "Little's", children ages 4-6 years. Having lost my natural Mother at the age of 8, I felt a strong connection to this program. My volunteering has definitely helped me, in addition to being a support for the children.

I did not love Girls' High but was grateful for the academic education I received. I did have many friends, but socially I felt uncomfortable and awkward amongst guys and did not date at all in high school. I was also a "goody-two-shoes" and stayed within my boundaries and did not test any limits. Clearly, today I am much more confident and self assured than I was in high school.

My twin sister, Renee, is my best friend, and despite the distance (she lives in NY) we communicate daily. Renee has always been there for me, literally from birth. We have shared lots of special moments together, both happy and sad - and will continue making many more memories together.

During these past several months, I have made a point of reaching out to others more often. While I read a lot of good books and enjoy watching some excellent programs on TV, I still long for more human connections. This is why I am happy to be involved with this GHS 212 project.

JANUARY 2021

We continue to remain in the midst of the pandemic, although it is a more promising time (health-wise) with the hope of getting the Covid vaccine. The New Year has begun and soon we will be turning the calendar to enter the 2nd month in the New Year. These days and weeks just ZOOM by! I continue to have LOTS of downtime to explore and think about the past years, while I rummage through boxes of keepsakes and collectibles.

I am forever grateful to reconnect with friends, former classmates, acquaintances, etc. Reaching out and establishing ties is wonderful and brings lots of joy and contentment for me.

My oldest granddaughter is enrolled in kindergarten this year and requested a picture of her mom (my daughter Debra) and me from our kindergarten years. I have been focused more on my years at GHS, so to think back to my elementary school days, was indeed a novelty and treat. I came across my class picture from the Pennell Elementary School. Of course, my twin Renee is in it. I recognize a few children, but I'm not certain what their names are. Definitely, there are some GHS ladies in this picture, but not sure who they might be.

During these past several months, while "quarantining" I have reflected a lot on my many life experiences (some joyous, and some not), and having this opportunity to share a nugget of my thoughts and feelings in my story with my 212 connections is very special. I look forward to sunshiny and non-pandemic days ahead when we are all living and enjoying the life of "post-vaccine" days!

Abington, PA
December 2020-January 2021

Carlotta Picazio Cundari

SO MANY WONDERFUL MEMORIES CLUTTER MY MIND as I begin to write down my thoughts. In retrospect, my experiences at GHS could only be described as a rescue and an awakening. I say so in retrospect because I began my term at GHS as a very angry 14-year-old girl. My life at home was not so easy. My dad was a compulsive gambler and my oldest brother was addicted to whatever drugs he could find on the street. In the middle of this mess, my sweet mother tried so hard to get me on a different path. I wanted to follow my favorite cousin, whom I idolized, to a private school in Germantown but there was no way we could afford that. Girls' High was the only option other than the South Philadelphia neighborhood high schools and Mom said no to those. I would be accepted into GHS if I could pass the entrance test and demonstrate that I did fairly well in elementary school. I succeeded on the former but because my eighth-grade teacher, Sister Patricia, considered any school that was not Catholic a heathen school, she refused to send my school records to GHS.

I remember speaking to a very kind Dr. Thompson (of course this first impression of her was not going to last very long) about my problem and she offered me an opportunity to take achievement tests so my academic skills could be determined. So, I angered Sister Patricia even more by getting accepted without her help. I distinctly remember getting on the subway that first day. My mother was with me because I think we were supposed to be together for orientation. I was angry... this is not what I wanted to do. At best, I wanted to go to Ancilla Domini with my cousin or to attend St. Maria Goretti high school with all of my neighborhood friends. I was not getting my way!

On that same subway was sweet faced Frances Cimino who came up to us and graciously asked if we were going to GHS. She said she wasn't with her mother because her mother had recently died and asked if she could ride with us. My anger at my mom at having to go to Girls' High began to lessen as I chatted with dear Franny. Life wasn't going to be so bad. I was able to open myself up a bit to this new experience with the help of my new friend. (Thanks Fran!)

Getting on that Broad Street subway every morning was a trip out of the world of narrow-minded nuns and family strife... It was one of the most important journeys of my life. Oh, that subway ride! The South Philly girls were fabulous... Franny, the Linda's, Anita, Elena, Helene, Katherine and Brenda... you knew and understood my experiences and also aspired to be something different from what the neighborhood could provide. Once we arrived at Broad and Olney our world opened wide.

I was in awe of how normal you all were and envisioned how just being there with you would make me normal too. I didn't feel competitive but maybe a bit jealous. You all dressed so well and were so experienced and intellectual and were so easy with each other. I was able to aspire to a better life in those pink marble halls. And a better life was granted to me. Using GHS as a launching pad I was able to achieve far more than I ever imagined possible... a wonderful life filled with a loving husband, two amazing daughters and five fantastic grandchildren, a rewarding career as a school principal, dear friends to share life's joys and sorrows, and amazing life experiences hiking in many parts of the world.

Over the years I've stayed in touch with a few of the subway girls, but it wasn't until our 40th reunion that I began to realize how much I wanted to reacquaint with all of you amazing women. That Broad Street hotel was a sea of brilliant happy women whom I needed and wanted to know once again. The busy part of life... the career building and the child raising was behind me. I had the time and desire to enrich my life with your lives. First, I reconnected with all of the subway girls and they continue to be a very special part of my life… my South Philadelphia sisters.

Then, thanks to Facebook I reconnected with many more of you. My love for Facebook is only great because it keeps me abreast of all of you and your wonderful lives and your brilliant opinions on whatever is the subject of the day. Now we are 70 and we are isolated and confined and your friendship and conversations never meant more to me. I continue to be so impressed with who you are and what you accomplished, and I am enriched by just knowing you. Before Girls' High I only knew white, Catholic people… a pretty limited life for sure. I needed to learn about what the rest of the world contained and GHS opened that door. I had never talked to a black person and never knew a Jewish person and I was ready to broaden my horizons with my first experiences at a temple, a Seder, a bat mitzvah, a Baptist funeral, the Philadelphia Orchestra, and a sweet sixteen party.

These were just a few events that began to let some daylight into my narrow world. Connecting once again with you refreshed in my mind how lucky I was to have been a Girls' High Girl. Here we are reflecting on our lives and sharing those reflections with interesting and interested women. Reaching out when this pandemic gets us down or wanting to know just how the joys and tragedies of life have left their marks or just what you are doing each day… it's grand. So here I am, a city girl born and bred, living a country life with working the land being one of my greatest joys. I would never have guessed this life for me but with an open mind anything is possible. Here I am, whereas the model of my parents' marriage was far from ideal, happily married for 48 years. Anything is possible. Here I am with my children and grandchildren living far away in Australia and Scotland and not being able to visit them except on FaceTime and I am okay with that because anything is possible. Yes, it all became possible because Girls' High opened me up and prepared me to face whatever life presents. Thank you, dear friends and dear school for my greatest gift…. a life well lived.

Toana, VA
December 2020

LONELINESS

Loneliness is when one feels left out.
It's the feeling of the aloofness of
    The people in one's surroundings.
Loneliness is being an outcast;
Not necessarily an outcast to society,
But more-so to one's friends.
Loneliness is being neglected by one's
    Family.
~~Loneliness is not being loved by any-~~
    ~~one.~~
Loneliness is not being able to find
    One's self.
I know, I am lonely.

                N. Marcelle Safra

                  2/24/66

Nona Safra

TEACHERS, MENTORS
AND INSPIRATION

IMAGINE GROWING UP IN A HOME WHERE DAUGHTERS have little or no value – the only purpose to aspire to in life was to marry well and bear grandchildren.

Then, at 13, the shock of finding something totally different could be had out of life, from the moment I entered those pink marble halls of Girls' High, and finding out that women could be more than breeders. It was truly shocking!

Here were teachers that expected us to go into the world and make it a better place and classmates whose families supported dreams of them becoming doctors, lawyers, academics and scientists among other careers. WOW! Girls who would go to college to do more than get their "MRS".

This was life changing . . .

And so was my beloved English teacher, the one and only Frankie Rubinstein who sat in front of each class on her stool and talked about life, men, our anatomy, love and sex. And, she did one hell of a job teaching English at the same time.

Whereas my home life sucked at the time, knowing that five days a week, within those four walls, I could answer questions (there were few wrong answers as long as you could justify your opinion), feel as though my life was meaningful and learn life lessons like being optimistic and living out dreams.

And, I learned to love classic literature. My sibling used the 'Cliff Note' version and scoffed that I was actually reading the books and spending time at Leary's bookstore. I was enthralled by the way authors painted scenery, people and moods with words. I still remember the characters in Hawthorne's "The Scarlet Letter" - Pearl, Dimmesdale, Chillingworth - and how those names were so descriptive. Then Frankie taught us about the bawdy Bard, William Shakespeare, which made his plays so much more interesting to read.

Best of all, she taught by example, which meant that I, too, could have a life to travel and live in places I dreamed about and do work I found exciting.

Her answers to simple questions were so direct. I expressed that being an attorney would be interesting and, where my parents' response was, 'why would you take a man's place in law school – he will need to support a family', dear Mrs. Rubinstein's face lit up and she became animated saying, 'Fabulous! And, you will be wonderful!'

From those experiences, I had my first encounters with feelings of self-esteem. And, most importantly, along the way, I learned that the subject matter was inconsequential as long as you knew how to pay learning forward to the next generation and beyond. Or in the words of the Bard, "It is not in the stars to hold our destiny but in ourselves."

After graduation, I succumbed to the life I was raised to live with a little of Frankie Rubinstein always rearing up. I married twice and had those grandbabies as expected but worked along the way. Some of the things I did were fun at the time like becoming one of the first female radio reporters in Philly – I didn't realize the significance until a young reporter here in Alaska thanked me for helping to break the 'glass ceiling' in newsrooms.

When we reconnected as the 212, I was struck by the careers and accomplishments of our 'sisters'. And, yet it was still the same intangible spirit of respect and sisterhood that we had in the 1960's going through civil rights, the war in Vietnam, assassinations, etc. Useless barriers that had existed between some of us in high school came down as we attended our 40th, 45th and 50th reunions and connected via Google groups, Facebook and Zoom. I now relish visiting my sisters of the 212 when traveling and discovering relationships with one another. My sisters of the 212. Mi familia!!!

After our 40th reunion I realized I was in a terrible relationship and needed to end it. My sisters were there by my side, with compassion and understanding but never judgment on the situation. And, when I finally separated from my husband, I was a guest for Passover that year in the home of Candy Whitman's sister (our beloved Audrey Whitman, 211) and her dear husband, Paul. And, emotional support from our class came through the front door with visits from our 'sisters' and we gathered in center city for lunch. It was so nurturing!

It was time to move on – but where? I visited my oldest friend, Rachel Stark Farrell, in California, then reconnected with Franny, Janice, Elaine and Theresa in Texas but neither place was 'it'. Then I found Alaska and, just like Frankie Rubinstein and the Bard said - "It is not in the stars to hold our destiny but in ourselves." So here I make my mark doing what we were inspired to do at GHS – make the world a better place. Here in the 'Last Frontier' or vast space with few two-legged occupants, those who have ideas for the betterment of Alaskans get to know each other rather quickly; so I was able to take the experiences of being an unwanted child, abuse and other social issues and be appointed to state boards and commissions on aging, disabilities, independent living and brain injury. It may have taken me longer to get here but, I'm here!

Some of the inspiration comes from the folks you meet (or encounter) along your journey. For me, working with the disabled was like meeting Helen Keller and Eleanor Roosevelt as a young child. It was rekindled by our 'sister' Robin Groth Michaelson who has graciously shared her daughter, Heather, and her accomplishments with us. All I have to do is see Heather's smile or the smile of the kids I advocate for to have a good day.

So, what have I learned in the fifty years since graduation? What has changed?

We now meet on Zoom as a group to deal with world events and the annus horribilis of 2020. What has blossomed is the honesty and openness in discussing our cultural, social and racial differences with depth and respect.

Though our lives had intertwined in the same city and time during high school, our individual lives were shaped by the diversity of families, places of worship and neighborhoods as well as race, religion, ethnic background, economic situation and familial circumstances. That new openness as well as maturity eliminated the need for 'the persona' some of us, including me, had taken on to cover our vulnerabilities. It is now okay to not be okay.

Now 'taboo' topics are put out there to be discussed with the maturity and raw emotions of 70-year-old women who have lived through so much and have the wisdom of being the 'village elders'. And, we've got plenty of time during the current pandemic to do this.

I've found inspiration from my 'sisters' sharing their experiences for me to be able to deal with heavier topics in my day-to-day life. Topics have included being a caregiver for a loved one with Alzheimer's, having an autistic grandchild, cancer, and dealing with death in the pandemic. Also, reminders that the best way to deal with political unrest is by getting active in the process, etc. And, plenty of feline time and pictures!

There are other topics we have touched upon over the years that I can see a benefit to revisit, maybe in smaller groups, such as rape, incest, alcoholism, child abuse, spousal abuse, elder abuse, the aging process, nursing homes, grandparents' rights and suicide (assisted or other).

And, I continue to be inspired. Frankie Rubinstein's influence and the humor of the 212 may help save local businesses during Covid in Homer Alaska aka the 'Cosmic Hamlet by the Sea' with a 'Cosmic Hamlet by The Sea' Festival where visitors can enjoy their "Gertrude Gimlet" along with the "Goodnight Sweet Prince" rate at a B&B and buying local honey products from our 'To BEE and Not to BEE" apiaries.

To my 212 sisters: We have much to share and learn from one another. You inspire me! Each day is a gift and I am thankful y'all are part of making mine wonderful!

Homer, AK
December 2020

Lily Samuel Rothman

THIS IS MY LIFE

I HAVE HAD IT EASY DURING THIS TIME OF COVID. I LIVE in Las Vegas and I do not gamble, but I feel quite lucky. My daughter and son-in-law have been here since May, so we always have stimulating company. They work in entertainment and comedy, so they are funny and continue to do virtual shows from our home. I can hug them any time I want. Through their theater, we have taken storytelling classes. This has caused me to contemplate and remember many things in my life - many happy, some sad and others life changing. We have Zoomed with friends, talking, drinking and playing games, and then we hear about black men being wrongly killed by police and my head erupts in angry feelings. We have virtual events through our community, such as bingo, game nights, and happy hours. And then there are wildfires in California displacing thousands, destroying homes, killing others and causing harm to the environment and wildlife, and I cry.

We are in a writing group, we have art Zooms, I create lots of stuff, I am a gourmet chef and have people to cook for. And then I think of those in the food industry who are struggling, people who are waiting in mile-long lines at food banks because they have no money. And those who are homeless, due to COVID 19, and I give money to help. I call people on the phone whom I love, and are alone, only able to do a drive-by or backyard get-togethers with their children and grandchildren, and I am saddened for them as I am grateful for my luck.

I also know that there are people in nursing homes who cannot see their families. This would have been me if this were two years ago. And I know the agony it would have been for me as it is now for them, being unable to comfort a loved and confused relative. I have run Zooms for my college class, and then think of all of the college students who are not able to have the fabulous college life I had because they can't reside on campus, must social distance and wear masks.

I started a havurah group, which means 'friend', at my Temple, and when we meet it is in a Zoom. As we don't know each other it is an artificial experience while we hope for a real encounter. My husband recorded choir music for our High Holiday services because they also were held on Zoom as singing together was, of course, not safe and not allowed. On Friday I bake a challah to help me feel closer to my Jewish faith as temples are closed and only the rabbi and cantor are there to lead as we stream the service.

I was just elected president of our community's art club and had to do the meeting via FaceTime because, while some of the officers were able to socially distance inside the art studio in our clubhouse, I am not ready to go inside the studio. We will be doing mostly virtual activities.

I am on a college committee to welcome incoming students; but when will they come on campus? And I am starting a college alumni group here in Vegas wondering when we will have a physical encounter.

I did a great deal of political work for Joe Biden, but I heard the worry in the voice of every supporter I called and realized how much I missed the physical voter contacts I had in elections past. Travel has been a huge part of our lives; so for every trip I have canceled, which of course makes me sad, I try to think of the future when I will be able to travel once again. Because now I think of the hotels, cruise lines, tour guides and dozens of others, who have few, to no one, using their services.

Yes, I have a great deal to be thankful for. But each thing is met with worry, concern, anger and frustration, and some hope that the vaccine will be distributed equitably and not cause more chaos. I know I must stay well and do everything I can do to not let this disease get me as we have dearest friends back in Philly who have not been so lucky. I am in the mourning process for one who died from COVID. I now can add myself to the hundreds of thousands who have lost someone in this pandemic. So, with this ever- changing world, I have a new fear. Donald Trump may run in 2024 unless Congress intervenes.

One thing I did, to keep myself engaged, and I thought, entertained, was to join Zooms from my Philadelphia High School for Girls Class. In doing that I have incurred the reliving of memories from a part of my life that was both happy and painful, exciting and scary, successful and demoralizing. My thought on first joining was that this was just going to be a social reunion, but by Zoom. I had not gone to reunions for years but went to my 50th just as we were finishing packing up our lives and memories of Philadelphia and moving. I really enjoyed seeing friends on what I knew was a superficial level. Of course, several of my lifelong friends have come from those four years and we are closer now than we had been, as COVID has caused us to want to stay connected through Zooms of ranting, gossiping and cooking together. In going on the GHS Zooms, I have let myself be swept up in the stories of women I didn't know well, but with whom I shared similar reactions and feelings of those four years. I came from about as sane a family as one can have. Yes, we had characters and things that were said and prejudices that I fought from the time I was very young, about 10 years old. This involved my refusing to speak to one of my grandmothers for at least six months due to some racist slurs she made. I remember yelling at my cello teacher in fifth grade for punishing another child whose offense I did not deem that horrific. And causing a scene at a water fountain labeled 'whites only' on a vacation in the South. And yes, screaming at my five-day-a-week art teacher at GHS for pandering to her pets and not getting herself back to view all of our projects. And then saying they were wrong after we worked on them for two weeks. In general, I always knew who I was and what was right, and while I had bullies in my life and suffered that, I bounced back. I was always very strong in character. For me, every day at GHS was a struggle. There were subjects in which I excelled, and those that ruined my GPA. Perhaps being an only child in a very small family made me more self-sufficient. I just think I'm the kind that has had to suck it up, get a grip and keep going. Those four years at GHS were my warrior years. I learned to battle it out for what I felt I deserved, not with the students, but with the faculty. When I left, I was ready for college and life.

My undergraduate years at Emerson College will always be four of the best of my life. My greatest life challenge was on 9/11 when my husband survived after walking down 74 flights after the first tower was struck. I often wonder if I could have physically walked down all of those stairs. But emotionally, I would have, because I had to. While he escaped, I stayed focused and calm. I was Nancy Drew, who was my childhood model of organization, planning and fearlessness.

This has been an emotional seesaw for me, but I learned many things. Finances were up and down but I learned not to worry. Getting food was solved by using technology. I don't need to shop in markets, I use Click List, drive over and my bags are brought out to the car and put in the trunk, or delivered. I could get addicted to this. By being nice and grateful, I even get staff in my CVS to run around getting me questionable essentials, such as boxes of hair dye, which wait for me at the counter. So finally, I don't dwell on what I have not been able to do; I think of what I will do. I encourage everyone to realize they will never have this type of free time again and to find a way to make good use of it. I make a point of watching comedy, not having violent shows on TV, listening to NPR and watching PBS. I cook amazing food and have baked more in this time than in my whole life before COVID-19. I choose to buy tickets to concerts, charities and auctions, and go on virtual tours of cities and museums so I can help others.

I see the light shining through this black hole, and while a vaccine for COVID is not going to be our final frontier, we have been where we have never been before and I say we have set a course going full speed ahead.

Las Vegas, NV
December 2020

Lois Sharp Rothenberger

I LOVE TO WALK. IT IS WHAT I DO. IT IS WHO I AM: A
walker, a hiker. According to my parents, I was older than the average
child when I finally stood and put one chubby leg in front of the other
while maintaining my balance. I suppose I have been trying to make up
for that late start ever since.

When I was frustrated at work, I slipped out of the office to take a
walk and sort out my thoughts. Raising teenage daughters as a single
mom often sent me to the streets of Mt. Airy to calm me down. And, weekend hikes along the trails in the Wissahickon chatting with close friends
were an important way I was able to bring balance to my life.

In 1992, I was diagnosed with breast cancer and required surgery,
radiation and chemotherapy over the course of a year. I had always
wanted to hike in the UK and my sister motivated me to rebuild my
strength so that we could plan a long-distance walk in 1994. The next
year was full of hikes and chats with my sister and then we boarded a
flight to London for our adventure. We tackled the Coast to Coast Trail
across northern England from the North Sea to the Irish Sea.

I was hooked on hiking adventures and have rarely had a vacation since that wasn't on trails. The next year I returned to the UK with
a co-worker and we met a British couple with whom we became fast
friends. We heard about their Ramblers Association of local walkers and
searched out groups in the States.

I found the Appalachian Mountain Club (AMC) and proceeded to
make more friends than you can imagine. Such an equalizer! No one
asked what you did for a living, where you reside, what car you drive
or any other status questions. Those things were often learned after a

while, but the initial conversations were all about the beauty you were experiencing, your gear, what you had packed for lunch, books you had read, places you had hiked.

When one of our classmates posted that her father had died, I realized that he had been a friend of mine in the AMC with whom I had hiked many times. He always enjoyed stopping at a diner for coffee and pie after a hike. Emily and I were able to celebrate his life with a hike together in Valley Forge Park.

I met another one of our classmates through work and we discovered that both of us are breast cancer survivors. Naturally, Margit and I teamed together to walk 60 miles in 3 days in a fundraising event. And yet another of our sisters became a regular participant in our Wednesday group hikes along the Delaware River. Such a joy to get reacquainted with Shirley and become friends with her husband, too.

On a day hike along the Appalachian Trail one March day in 1999 I met a lovely man. He admired my jacket, and I loved his boots. We were off and running! Or walking. My wonderful husband, Alan. We camped and hiked and fished. We bought a cabin on a river in the wooded mountains of north central Pennsylvania and led many hiking weekends for the AMC.

We explored walking paths in the UK, Spain, France, Italy, Switzerland, Austria, Slovenia, Canary Islands and more. We "bagged" the highest peaks in Scotland, England, and Wales. We circumnavigated Mont Blanc walking through three countries and clambering over many mountain passes. We loved traveling to the west and discovering the hidden treasures in the Rocky Mountains. Endless adventures, endless fun. And, always with so many friends and many more added every year. Magical. And, it all came from a love of walking.

And then on Christmas Day of 2018, Alan wasn't feeling well and I took him to the ER. He died only three days later from a rare and aggressive form of leukemia. Just two weeks before he was as physically active as always and losing him was a shock. Of course, my family was wonderful and supportive but I cannot overemphasize the AMC "family" and how those continued walks with friends buoyed me.

However, I found that no matter how I love walking and how many supportive friends there were, I was not able to "move on". Grief totally filled me, and I was no longer a walker, but a widow, a griever, a woman in pain. But, I did manage to put one foot in front of the other and "move forward" with that pain and grief. And, as I have moved forward, my life has grown even though the grief has not diminished. Instead, continuing to be on the trail has made my life bigger so that the grief now has a cushion around it and it is not the only thing I have.

See you on the trail!

North Wales, PA
January 2021

Rachel Stark Farrell

"JOHNNY IS COMING TO VISIT! AND HE'S BRINGING Sean," I was exclaiming to any of my friends at Girls' High who would listen. I could see them giving each other the 'side eye' and thinking I was simply delusional. What 30-year-old married man would drive from San Francisco to Philadelphia with his 3 year old son to visit me, a high school senior misfit?

I had slogged my way through three years of the Philadelphia High School for Girls, grudgingly attending summer school as though it was a natural extension of my education: Algebra I, French I; Geometry, French II; Algebra II, French III... If I had just attended school every day, I probably could have kept up, but I dreaded those pink marble halls. Allegedly, one needed a certain IQ to even be accepted, but my sister who was one year ahead and my mom and my aunt were alumni, so I assumed I was really allowed entry for that reason, not my IQ. I was already convinced that I was destined for mediocrity. In my freshman year, I set my sights on participation in Contest, but alas (!) my grades didn't meet the GPA requirement. Everything was so regimented. Dr. Faust had been teaching when my mom and aunt had attended, some 30-40 years prior, for Pete's sake!

Even then, I was a free spirit. I despised the daily routines. Each morning I sabotaged my intention to make it to school by stopping at Danny's Restaurant for my daily breakfast (Pepsi and fries) and if anyone even hinted at cutting school, I was a willing and eager partner. We'd spend the days at the art museum or public library or just hanging out at Rittenhouse Square.

Although I wasn't part of any particular crowd, I had many friends, all of whom were part of other groups, probably from wherever they had attended junior high. I didn't really know anyone in Girls' High from my neighborhood, the Northeast, except Nona, and her parents forbade her from hanging out with me since my parents were social activists. As a union organizer, my mom had even joined the Communist Party during the McCarthy era. My closest friends were Candy and Rhea. I spent any weekend that they allowed at their houses. I have such warm memories of Candy's house, her kind and generous mom, Sonja, and the free-standing chess table where we would challenge each other, the dancing to Motown in her bedroom and Candy keeping me constantly entertained with her dry wit that so few could match. I shared a small bedroom with my sister in our tiny apartment and Candy's and Rhea's homes represented luxury that I had never experienced. I was close with Kat and Carla, Psylvia, Nora, Freda and Wendy, Madeline and many others but never had that intimacy during high school that I had with Candy and Rhea. Rhea carried a trauma from her mom's death that at times felt haunting.

My parents, probably at their wits' end, after my third summer school session, decided to send me to visit my mom's cousin and her creepy husband in Northern California. They owned a chicken ranch about an hour north of San Francisco. The wife would leave for work in the city every morning and I'd wake up to him in my bed. Did I mention they were in their late 50's? I was still a virgin, probably not believable with my mini skirt, boots, twiggy haircut and sassy attitude, but true. They too were Communists and in a stroke of luck (or fate), they introduced me to young Communists in Berkeley who invited me to stay with them and their two young children. I loved little kids and landed right in my element and away from the pervert.

So, this young couple, Bobby and Larry, took me to the first ever *Be In*, in Berkeley. It just blew me away. Live music, free food and everyone smoking pot and hash or on mushrooms or acid. Suddenly, they saw folks they knew, Johnny and his wife, Susie and their two younger kids

Ginny and Sean. We sat on their blanket and I locked eyes with Johnny and I swear, I fell instantly in love. There was some ancient and mystical connection that took us to a different time and universe. Johnny mentioned that they had just rented a flat in the Haight Ashbury and would be moving in soon. We parted ways with no plan to meet again.

Meantime, Rhea had told me that she would also be in San Francisco, visiting her cousin Frank. We connected a couple of times and after she left I called Frank to meet up. He also lived in the Haight. We were strolling all over Golden Gate Park and the Panhandle, live music everywhere, and I was telling him all about this guy Johnny I had met and fallen madly in love with, when we happened into the "I and Thou" cafe and there was Susie. "Where is your beautiful husband?" I asked with my usual unfiltered candor. "Oh, he took some acid and is wandering around somewhere," she responded. "Oh. Well this is Frank. Frank, meet Susie." Who knew what an auspicious meeting this would be. Johnny returned. It seemed fated since we'd had no plan to meet again. I needed to be back to my cousins' house, so they decided to drive me. Susie drove (obviously) and Frank came along with the kids hopping around in the very back of the station wagon. When we arrived at my cousins' and introductions were made, they were delighted to find out that Susie was the daughter of Hon and Archie Brown, the most well known and active Communists in the Bay Area.

I reluctantly went back to Philly to finish high school with the solemn oath to move to San Francisco as soon as I graduated. Johnny called me faithfully and now he and Frank had decided to drive to Philly to see Rhea and me. And they were bringing Sean. For real.

When Johnny pulled up to the curb at Girls' High to pick me up after school, my friends' mouths were agape. They had never seen a hippie. No one in Philly had. Long hair and a beard was for vagrants only. Now it was a thing. I loved shocking everyone I knew. And the vindication that he was real, and had driven across the country to profess his love for me, made me feel like a rock star. I finally had value.

The rest is history, to be saved for a book or maybe some later chapters in this or another compilation. Briefly, I dropped out of Girls' High because I couldn't graduate with my class since I needed summer school as usual (trigonometry and French IV). I was really torn about dropping out so I went to my favorite teacher, Frankie Rubinstein, for her guidance. "Follow your heart," she advised. She was a kindred free spirit and the wisest person I knew. I guess I was just going to her for confirmation to follow my dream.

So off to the Haight I went, moving into the commune with Johnny and Susie. She and Frank were already lovers but with 17 people living together, it was a free for all, truly another chapter unto itself. I had our first son in San Francisco at Mt. Zion hospital, a traumatic event, so when I was going to give birth to our second child (we lived in Humboldt by then) I decided to have her at home. All of my friends and neighbors came to watch and when they all soon became pregnant they asked me to be their midwife.

Madeline, with whom I had remained close, came out to visit and was witness to Sita's birth. She later moved to Humboldt.

Years later, we sold our house in Humboldt and moved into a school bus. By then I was pregnant with our fourth child. Sean had always lived with us and the girls had lived with Susie. We decided to get land together so we could have all of the kids in one place. So we bought 10 acres in Nevada County, CA, Susie on one side and Johnny and me on the other. We built a little shed next to the bus to have a place to dry our weed. Everyone in rural Northern California was pot farmers, with us being no exception. In fact, if I need a claim to fame, it might be that this is the thing I do the best.

A couple of years after we had our 5th child, Johnny took up with another woman (it certainly wasn't the first time). He left us, taking the bus. We moved into the drying shed and lived off the grid for years to come, cooking and heating our home with a wood stove and using kerosene to study as I had taken the GED, attended Yuba College an hour away and was accepted to Stanford University's Physician Assistant Program.

My long and tortuous marriage to Rick and the relationships I built with his six kids, is again, another chapter. I went on to open a medical clinic, and birth center, incorporating my core values of social justice and equity for staff and patients, which has now grown into four sites of a Federally Qualified Health Center, where I serve as CEO. I have 15 grandchildren (13 grands and 2 great-grands) and my beautiful home on those same 10 acres, now with electricity! I have been extremely fortunate, and although I am single, my life is extraordinarily full and complex.

My old friendships, especially with Candy and Madeline remained intact over the years. Although I didn't regularly speak with Rhea, I was devastated, but not really surprised, by her suicide. I became friends with Ellen and Jackie when visiting Candy in Paris, which I did a few times, as well as in Barcelona. However, it was our 40th reunion that was really transformational. I met scores of women I hadn't known in high school or didn't remember, but the after party at Audrey Whitman's house, sealed these lifelong relationships.

These Zoom calls we attend have given me so much pause to reflect, to look at my implicit biases, to feel like I have shared teen experiences with others who never showed how much they too were suffering. Now, as wise old women, we have the depth and capacity and trust in each other to do that deep dive that has become true intimacy. I feel like I have so much in common with these adult women, politically, spiritually and shared values that frankly, I wish I had known them better throughout the years. We still are young and active enough to plan a gathering after Covid and I look forward to that time greatly. In the meantime, sharing our stories is a marvelous way to continue to build these friendships. I look forward to the next chapter of our stories, literally and figuratively.

Nevada City, CA
December 2020
www.myharmonyhealth.org

Ruth Stark

ON COMING OF AGE
(70, THAT IS)
IN THE TIME OF COVID-19

UNLIKE MANY OF MY PEERS, I FOUND MYSELF HAPPILY ensconced in my professorial job of 40 years as the virtual calendar page turned to 2020 and I confronted the approach of my 70th birthday. Not only did I mentally note its occurrence in the latter part of the year (September), but I took care to remind myself that it would occur toward the end of that month (September 22nd). As a passionate biophysicist leading research that spans the animal, plant, and fungal kingdoms and a professorial mentor to scores of students from high school to postdoctoral levels, I was also relishing the end of a three-year term as Chair of my department at The City College of New York (CCNY) and anticipating my first-ever year long sabbatical. I looked forward to planning, supervising, speaking and writing – preferably in an array of exotic locales – as well as blowing off uninteresting meetings and boorish people, getting more serious about healthy physical activities, and (perhaps) devoting serious thought to how I would transition into retirement.

By February of 2020 I was reading with horror the first million-size projections of CoViD-19 deaths in the U.S. On March 6th I went to see a West Side Story revival on Broadway – the house was packed. By March 20th my CCNY colleagues and I had closed down our laboratories and moved our instruction entirely to remote mode, followed by a hiatus of 3+

months that has not yet recovered beyond 25% occupancy. I stuck with my sabbatical plans in order to decompress and Zoomed my students toward their publications and degrees, but how to raise fresh research funds when you're eating down your budget by paying people who cannot work productively? Bad luck, but not much recourse. Was this the time to let those retirement thoughts return to the fore? Would I be forced to confront retiring as a fade-out rather than an affirmative choice? Seemed like an unpalatable scenario.

Though I have fulfilled just a sliver of my year's aspirations, and my retirement plan has financial underpinnings but still lacks substance, I have reached a kind of reflective inflection point on the run-up to a year's worth of abnormal life in CoViD Times. And thanks to our Google Group and Writing Project, Girls' High is an unanticipated but important element of this story. As a science nerd, in 1968 and still now, I made an organized list of how I reached this hard-to-acknowledge milestone in 2020 and floated into 2021.

1. I am making scheduling choices that acknowledge my preferences more honestly than in the Before Times. Yes, I could doom scroll and Zoom all day every day, but it has become my habit to ramp up gradually while in my bathrobe, entertain a distracting headline or email, buckle down to handle something more demanding of my brain, then make breakfast and take a shower before diving in again. It's an unplanned alternative to rushing out of my apartment to a firehose of appointments – so why not proceed this way every day?! Deprived of access to my busy workplace, I equipped a sequestered basement workspace, surrounded by the buzz and bubble of eight turtles and 20 fish and opening into the quiet lower-level patio of a townhouse backyard. If this is isolation, it is also a clarifying preparatory exercise for more serious analytical and emotional challenges. It has allowed me to join discussions of new scientific forays by scientists around the world, flesh out my own quirky ideas, learn about why people eschew vaccines and how mutant viruses could evade

them, take a break for a mini Yiddish lesson or a Klezmer music concert before swapping back to the macromolecular glories of virulence factors in pathogenic fungi.

2. In almost any weather (spurred on by the electronics on my wrist), regardless of pending deadlines, I walk for 30-60 minutes each day. For someone who disliked sports and never joined a gym, this is a big deal. Though it has been lovely to walk to work these past 3+ years, I now walk for the joy of exploring and observing. The parks are glorious even when I get turned around and need to find a tall building to get straight: the Harlem Meer, the Conservatory Garden, Morningside and Marcus Garvey Parks. Inventive outdoor dining structures and New York Restaurant Week take-out style. Lee-Lee's 'Rugelach by a Brother.' Of course there are also shut-down restaurants and desperate folks lingering on some street corners. I love NYC even more than before, but will its future be reimagined with a greater degree of equity or a broader demographic, or simply fewer resources?

3. THINGS that matter, those that don't matter anymore, those that matter more now. As I look back, I took pride in academic achievement at Girls' High, but I thought we were filling our heads with facts while the Central boys were learning to think. I chafed when Mrs. Gitman punished me for improperly placed footnotes but chuckled when she asked me to explain Economics to my classmates. I never earned the respect I craved from Mrs. Yeager for my scientific promise, but does it matter a fig now that I've had a successful and fulfilling career? Dr. Thompson warned me that if my behavior did not improve, I would be excluded from the school's honor awards (horror!). Those THINGS mattered to her when she blackballed me as a troublemaker on my college applications, but it's immaterial now. I only valued Mr. Edelson and Mrs. Byers long after their English

classes were over, when I discovered myself as a scientist who can also write and speak skillfully. I was wounded for quite some time after failing to become the first tenured woman faculty member in an all-male Chemistry department at Amherst College, but I never let those bastards see me cry. By taking my know-how and grant money to a new academic venue, cultivating some work-life balance, and engaging with a healthier professional network, I was able to build a more exciting academic career and have a family on the back end of that debacle.

4.   PEOPLE who matter, perhaps more than ever because we cannot see them maskless in three dimensions. Dear friends who had fallen out of touch or were worried about everyone living in NYC. Former lovers; subsequent lovers of my former lovers now deceased. Friends doing Zoomed memorials for those lost to CoViD or cancer or who-knows-what. Former grad school classmates and students I taught 40 years ago. My precious grown-up child on the threshold of an independent career in Astrophysics… but currently holed up in Queens in a mother-in-law's basement.

5.   And of course the ladies of the Swelvers and the broader 212 Class of Girls' High, whom I was fortunate to reconnect with at our 40th reunion and a bit thereafter. After so many years and so little contact, I never imagined how easily I would reconnect with women I last saw as 17-year-olds squished into an arcade photo booth. How delighted I would be to encounter classmates since elementary school, fellow student activity devotees, and acquaintances who simply sat in the next seat at school. What a blast I would have with a magnificently diverse crew at a mini reunion in Paris! I regret that I knew so few of you deeply; I was surely oblivious to the difficulties that some of you endured during our high school time together. Nonetheless, rediscovering you as strong, mature women is an inspiring delight. I didn't want

to read many of your stories until I had drafted my own, but now I am gobbling them up each day. Ironically, this is a pleasure that seems enhanced by our current pandemic circumstances. The ties that bind us, both retrospective and prospective, will hopefully flourish – through speech, in writing, and by hugging in person -- in the times ahead.

New York, NY
February 2021
https://resgroup.ccny.cuny.edu/

Medellin Stephens

A JOURNEY IMMERSED
IN KNOWLEDGE

LISTENING CAN BE A QUIET, ANONYMOUS ACTIVITY perfect for garnering information. So, I sat listening, my first meeting with new and previously involved high school classmates invited to write and share life experiences.

At 70 looking back at myself in high school, I was so definite in opinions and feelings though our world was just cracking open. From high school we would begin to move through life situations that would expand our perceptions. Truths carried us forward, but later we might find, we missed the sweetest one. So, it was on this day I sat listening to my classmates, until at one point several commented on how fortunate they had felt receiving an education at Girls' High. The criteria for entering this public school were not bound by culture, race or religion but academic standing.

My first impression of life was books, being read to, and words. Everyone in my family seemed, to me, to be a teacher, and their friends were teachers too. Hence, homework had rules - no television during the school week, interactive preparation for tests, and checking that homework was completed. To escape when no adult was around, I would place a book between a textbook and appear to be studying. I do not remember any of this as arduous or disciplinary. It was what it was. Then one day, my aunt who taught at Masterman, a demonstration school, told me I would be going to school with her. The simple explanation, I was declining academically. There was no scolding or theatrics and this move did indeed, right the situation. However, the agony of my father's sister having daily access to my life felt, at times, embarrassing, observational, and too personal. Though there were wonderful moments too: helping with bulletin boards or being given, by the teacher across the hall from my aunt, my first thesaurus.

When I graduated I chose a college in the Midwest, distancing from family and East Coast life.

A degree in philosophy and religion with a minor in English did not provide a definitive choice of careers, so for support in going out into the world, I went off to Rhinelander, Wisconsin with a friend who would be assisting in a school where her aunt taught.

Memories fade but some remain tangible and accessible, marking significant moments. A day filled with sun. Houses, next to but above me crowded with flowers. A random unexpected thought. There must be more to life than what I'm doing. Yet, what that more was, I didn't know, but I was determined to find out. And where had that thought come from? Perhaps dormant but nurtured by my degree, or spurred by participation in encounter and sensitivity groups in college. One time sitting in a room silently facing someone asking, "who are you?" repeatedly, to which we were instructed not to reply, shook me deeply.

Fortunately, the answer to the "what more?" was provided by some- one we did not yet know. The ICU nurse on the floor where I worked as ward clerk suggested we might want to connect with her daughter, who was our age. She was, it turned out, hoping to form a class to bring in a teacher so her parents could learn meditation. In the end my friend and I joined. This was a turning point for us. Most miraculously for me because the weekend after I learned, my contentious relationship with the head nurse where I worked as a ward clerk disappeared, as if it had never existed. At home we meditated morning and evening, preparing for the day and renewing our energy for a productive evening. Where we had been tired, we were alert - a miracle caused by closing the eyes, experiencing awareness and deep rest simultaneously, a state of restful alertness. Here was a technique of inner knowledge to complement the outer knowledge of a changing world. I grabbed on and for eight years, I taught Transcendental Meditation and in Fairfield, Iowa received an MA from Maharishi International University in Higher Educational Administration, a merging of education and universal knowledge.

I used to tell my family I would never become a teacher, and then one day realized that teaching meditation contradicted this edict, and I thoroughly demolished it once I began teaching ESL classes to college students.

When I left Taiwan and came to Hawaii my life transitioned again and through a series of situations I found myself teaching the Art of Living. It was an emotional transition since I thought I would never move from the path I was on, but I was learning one of the first statements from Maharishi, "the relative (relative life) is always changing." My tendency in life was to hold on to what was and resist change. Slowly life was showing me its impermanence, that it was not about stability but inner equanimity. That is, that moving through change smoothly was possible. This experience was not spontaneous, but instead was a growing awareness. Sri Sri Ravi Shankar says that with awareness change has already begun.

Education, to me, should develop the foundation for inquiring, curious, creative, open minds. When young children were taught a standard curriculum using three different methods, all succeeded. The common denominator was attention and love that made students blossom. Girls' High gave me a strong educational foundation and the skills needed to succeed in college. Coming to gratitude for an aunt who, despite my attitude and reactions, made sure I received the best education, was a realization from participating in this project. From contention to understanding to gratitude and a piece of life resolved. But the question of "who am I" requires another kind of knowledge and experience. Love grows us, but to know we are love expands us, and contains the possibility of expanding and changing the world. I have been fortunate that my life in knowledge has been two-fold, of the changing world and the non-changing self, and gratitude embraces both.

For Now, TX
January 2021
https://www.knectingstories.com/

Robin Thomas Poponne

HAIL ALL HAIL

THE COVID PANDEMIC HAS FOUND ME, AT TIMES, FEEL-ing lonely, anxious, and totally frustrated with the plight of this planet. However, once again, my high school community has contributed to the alleviation of some of my stress, while catapulting me further into the 21st century. While attending the Philadelphia High School for Girls (Girls' High), I learned to drive and type on a keyboard. Years later, my classmates invited me to join Facebook, just prior to our 45th class reunion. In 2020, members of my class were invited to meet through Zoom technology during the pandemic. I learned how to mute and unmute, chat, and raise or lower my virtual hand. I felt less alone and less disconnected as a result of these technological advances.

My first connection with my Girls' High community was as a 12-year-old freshman. I started first grade at age 5 and 1/2 and I completed a program in junior high that combined seventh and eighth grades into one year. I wanted so much to "fit in" but my mother made me wear a pink organza dress with a velvet bow on my first day. I protested that it made me look like a child and she answered, "you are still a 12-year-old." I tied a cardigan around my waist in an attempt to lessen the damage. I worked hard to hide my age only to have the *Iris* (school newspaper) announce on the front page that I was one of two 12-year-olds in our class.

Still, I had little to worry about. My friends at Girls' High were such a diverse group of teen-age girls, that it was not hard for me to fit in.

Because I was only 12, I did a lot more observing than leading in the social arena. The girl-talk in the locker room gave me vicarious views that I would replay later in life, when I was ready. I was able to celebrate my own uniqueness and be comfortable being who I was, even as I was becoming who I am. My yearbook autographs were evidence to friends: Black, White, Asian, super brains, super laid back, quiet, raucous, funny, and artistic. There was Lauren, whose father owned a funeral home and who used to take us there after school to hang out. There was the folk music club, the Star Trek/Spock Fan Club, and my chance to portray Uhura (Who-Are-Ya) in the "Frolic" play, *Intangible Spirit*. In junior and senior year, it was all about the two Judys (Judith Welch and Judy Wong) who taught me what friendship was all about as we rambled the halls and the city, traveling to Chinatown or down to Rittenhouse Square to hang out with other flower children. There was also the traditional world of majorettes and cheerleaders. Being active helped me out on class trips; to the zoo where I had to outrun a peacock, and to Washington D.C., where I outran our vice principal who wanted to pull me out of an anti-Vietnam rally.

I had many wonderful teachers, especially in English, geometry, chemistry and Latin. However, I learned more about myself because I was in a safe environment that allowed me to grow and explore. I learned that I had the will and the discipline to complete challenging tasks. I learned to focus and wisely choose my environmental influences; to have courage to face my weaknesses and ask for help when needed; to reach beyond the surface and dig deeper; to manage time although I was a hurry-up-and-wait kind of person; and to have patience and trust in my teachers and family who constantly told me I would have plenty of time to travel, to decide what I wanted in life, and to know how I would make a difference in this world.

All was not perfect. I was often confronted (more so by faculty than students) with racial prejudice: from my counselor and a teacher who told me I was not good enough to be admitted to a Seven Sisters school (one of the East Coast's consortium of distinctive colleges for women);

to the teacher who looked at me each day as if I had two heads because I dared to ask in which part of the year we would study Africa in world history class. I felt tremendous pressure from my parents to succeed and grades below a B were unacceptable. When this history teacher gave me a D for my first report card, issued just before my birthday, my father shaped my birthday cake into a large D. That grade never appeared on my report card again.

I had supportive schoolmates and family to get me past these upsets. As a class, we had our share of traumas. We lost Sherrie Harabin to an alleged campus suicide and our graduation followed a tumultuous spring tainted with the assassinations of Robert Kennedy and Martin Luther King Jr. Somehow, we persevered and supported each other.

We were all women in process, in various stages of development. Some had a very clear sense of their futures and some, like me, did not have a clue where this animated contrivance called destiny, who grabbed people by the collar, was about to take us. Although sometimes my inner low self-esteem talk attempted to take control of my teenage mind and body, I was, nevertheless, a member of the class of '68. We were smart, determined, soul and heart-strong, and we would rock the world.

Despite my counselor's stinging words, I secretly applied and was accepted to Smith College where I met many women whose brains gave them superpowers in any arena. But while I was catching up socially and raising my fragile sense of self-esteem in the land of Julia Childs and Gloria Steinem, I held my own because I was a Girls' High girl. I had the tools required to succeed anywhere. Nonetheless, I missed my high school sisters. Eventually, I could walk through the City Hall courtyard under the Billy Penn statue and no longer run into a familiar face. I held onto the last vestige; a *Life* Magazine with an iconic photo of my classmate, Psylvia, dancing at the Woodstock Festival. I applauded her for her more than fifteen minutes of fame and remembered many carefree conversations with her in the pink marbled halls. I also, much to the chagrin of my daughter, loudly sang the school song each time I drove by. I discovered, after the date, that there had been a 10-year reunion for my class. My mother had thrown out the information. "You graduated from college", she said. "Why would you need to go to a high school reunion?" She just did not understand!

I went on to teach in Nigeria, New York, D.C., and the U.S. Virgin Islands. I was a charter member of four dance companies in New York, St. Croix, and in the Baltimore/ Washington D.C. area. I later became a dance-movement therapist in the Maryland Behavioral Health System. I was twice married (also twice divorced) and raised a daughter. One morning, I answered a call-waiting signal and a voice asked, "Are you Robin Thomas?" I had not heard that last name in many years. It was Emily Kahn Freedman. She apologized for not trying the number sooner, in time for the 40th reunion. She invited me to join the class Facebook page and to attend a luncheon. Suddenly, I was reconnected! Through mini-reunions in Paris with Ellen Williams Lebelle and Gail Berlin, Barcelona with Candace Whitman, and the 45th and 50th reunions, I gained and regained friendships with women I intend to remain in touch with through the rest of my life. I was once again, a member of a tribe of women who accepted me for who I was. I did not have to prove myself and I was free to express my opinion and share my projects.

I loved seeing and hearing about who we had become, not only professionals, doctors, educators, politicians, comediennes, movie production moguls, and scientists, but also pageant finalists, rescuers of bees and the planet, partners, wives, mothers, grandmothers, writers, and artists in bloom.

I was saddened to learn of the personal traumas experienced by many of my classmates. In a women's workshop I once attended, the speaker instructed us to look to the left and look to the right and note that one or two of us were very likely victims of abuse.

Covid tried its best to shut us all down and some of us are hurting from the loss, the isolation and limitations (not all of us are retired). Our high school class Zoom sessions have become safe and necessary spaces for us to share our grief as well as our triumphs. I applaud the courage of all of us who could bring ourselves to these Zoom sessions.

I wish we could reach more of our classmates who may be hurting, busying themselves with the hard tasks of living through a pandemic. I would want them to know that Zoom time is not just a frivolity but a gift to ourselves, our past and present selves, and an opportunity to check in and be checked in on.

We rant, we rave, we cry, and we laugh together, still soul and heart strong.

These gatherings help me to realize that we are still coming together from all walks of life and can appreciate each other more deeply than the surface of status, success, or lifestyle. After the death of George Floyd, we discussed racial injustice from different perspectives. There are those of us who lived all of our lives with the footprint of racism on our necks and backs and those who are just coming into awareness and who are reaching out for guidance on their personal journeys.

Experience plus intelligence does mean wisdom and so we share – from the learned details of Corona, to insights into political sci-fi Trump style, to events with our spouses, partners, and grandchildren. We share! It is said all we needed to know we learned in kindergarten but the gifts we get in high school can become life-long treasures.

212th class – rock on!

Baltimore, MD
December 2020

IN MY SOUL ETUDE

I have no one to play with so I play on words
Pandemic pandemonium has me stressed out, stretched out of sorts
Doing cat stretch yoga with my pet can't hit all the right places

Isolated without a soulmate cellmate, I sing a soul etude
What do you get when you kiss a guy? Enough germs to catch Corona
And when you do, he'll never phone ya.

In my country, my hood, my TV there is no justice, just us
No, just me
Alienation, alien nation, bio terrorism's current alias is Covid

And I feel so I-soul-lated
Not yet inoculated

Fully incorporated into I Mac culture in my house immaculate
But my social life's a mess

Often irate, but struggling to remember "I rate"
Incarcerated, no plane to catch
But we will catch up someday, won't we??

Baltimore, MD
February 2021

Diana White Sims

THE OPENING SENTENCE IN CHARLES DICKENS' NOVEL
A TALE OF TWO CITIES, reminds me of my life when I entered Girls' High in September 1964. Charles Dickens wrote "It was the best of times, it was the worst of time, it was an age of wisdom, it was the age of foolishness..." Girls' High is a magnet school in the School District of Philadelphia with a competitive admissions process. I was a foster child transplanted from Baltimore, Maryland to live with some very distant relatives. It was not the best home experience, but as foster care goes it was not the worst. The family was educated, attended church and was considered significant in their circle. But I always felt like an outsider and missed the warm fuzzies of being raised by loving parents. Being accepted into Girls' High was an honor even though I was not so aware of it during that time. The school's motto was Vincit qui se vincit (she conquers who conquers herself).

Girls' High offered an excellent opportunity for learning, as well as an array of traditional events. My classmates added to the fun. Contest was exciting. I was not very athletic, but I enjoyed watching the other girls compete. County Fair was always fun with the food, games and entertainment. The Holiday Show and performance of Treble Clef made our school special. We had enriching clubs and a variety of other activities. I was a member of the Future Teachers and Homemaker of America Clubs. All of the programs, clubs and unique activities made our school special even though it was more special for some than others.

The world was different outside of those pink marble halls, but partly due to Girls' High and my classmates I had a foundation to stand on. There was racial unrest and gross misconduct at the highest level of government. There were healthcare, education, and employment inequities as well as environmental concerns. I mainly lived in that outside world. I protested and marched in the streets of Philadelphia. I gave out flowers and wore a button that said "make love not war". I did not quite understand the full meaning of the slogan at the time. I ran an African Boutique, made dashikis, knitted kufis and I made jewelry out of dried beans. I taught African history to kids on the porches of Germantown. I sold clothes and AVON door to door. I went to meetings and listened to discussions about the pending revolution. I volunteered to help fix up houses in the inner city and attended leadership training through the Y teen program. We had basement parties and we danced in the street. In contrast, I watched my friends go off to Vietnam with some never returning or returning much different than when they left.

My life was different from many of my classmates who lived in grand houses, had warm loving parents or celebrated their 16th birthday with a big party. I feel comfortable in saying many of my classmates were not aware of the life I lived outside of those marble halls. Nor were they aware of the life of people of color during that time.

The more things change, the more they remain the same yet there are always some things that are just a little different. We are still experiencing racial unrest and gross misconduct in the highest level of government. There are still healthcare, education and employment inequities a well as environmental concerns. I am still very socially conscious. I volunteer along with my sorority Alpha Kappa Alpha to uplift the lives of people, mainly in one of the poorest communities in Baltimore City. We target education, healthcare, history, political consciousness and homelessness. I support voter education and historically black colleges and universities (HBCUs).

The difference is I am no longer 17. I am 70 now. I have furthered my education beyond high school. I have married and divorced. I have given birth to two children and I play an active role in my grandchildren's lives. I have experienced the highs and lows of just living. I understand so much more than I did then. I have overcome many of my shortcomings and believe I can control my emotions and subsequent behaviors. I am living our motto "Vincit qui se vincit". Girls' High and the Class of 212, thank you for the foundation.

Joppa, MD
January 2021

acyrologia

An incorrect use of words - particulately replacing one word with another word that sounds similar but has a diffident meaning - possibly fuelled by a deep-seeded desire to sound more educated, witch results in an attempt to pawn off an incorrect word in place of a correct one. In academia, such flaunting of common social morays is seen as almost sorted and might result in the offender becoming a piranha, in the Monday world, after all is set and done, such a miner era will often leave normal people unphased. This is just as well sense people of that elk are unlikely to tow the line irregardless of any attempt to better educate them. A small percentage, however, suffer from severe acyrologiaphobia, and it is their upmost desire to see English used properly. Exposure may cause them symptoms that may resemble post-dramatic stress disorder and, eventually, descend into whole-scale outrage as they go star-craving mad. Eventually, they will succumb to the stings and arrows of such a barrage, and suffer a complete metal breakdown, leaving them curled up in the feeble position.

Candace Whitman

WOMAN'S HIGH
A WHITMAN SAMPLER

THERE IS A WONDERFUL GERMAN WORD *"FERNWEH"*, which I've always loved - and always missed in other languages. It's the opposite of homesickness (i.e., *"Heimweh"*). Translated literally, it's "faraway sickness": the longing for distant places, for the unknown, the yet unexperienced. What a wonderful word, absent in English. The yearning for the yonder, the ache for away. I've suffered from that malady since I was a child. I think it was kindled when my parents took off with 10-year-old me (along with one-year-older sister and one-year-younger brother) to spend three aimless months wandering around Europe – no hotel reservations, no pre-booked guided tours, no scheduled circuit – just an itinerant family of 5, in a Peugeot station wagon (but half the size of a Chevy sedan) bought the first week in Paris, stumbling haphazardly from one exciting new experience to the next - wayward wayfarers from Wissahickon, traipsing through France, Italy, Switzerland, England, Holland. That ignited the fire, the *Fernweh* – and the deep urge to one day find my way back to Europe, with all those strange languages, strange streets, strange buildings, strange foods, and even stranger people. I was ten years old and hooked.

Three years later: first baby steps at GHS. I loved it immediately–basically because of one Kathleen O'Neill. How lucky can one get in life? My new stumbled-upon friend is cool and colorful, funky and funny, iconoclastic and iconic - and one of the greatest prizes of my life -- at that time bundled together with Anna Swora, Rachel Stark, Carla Rappaport, Nora Solomon, Kat Flynn and Danny's Soda Shop. And even the peripheral girls I happily still grazed from elementary school: Andrea Block, Judy Lipshutz, Cynthia Doty, Marguerite Bracy, Greta Gordon, Marsha Kramer, Sharon Franz, and a whole bunch more. I was surrounded by gurlfriends - amiEs, FreundINnen, amigAs, amigUEs, amiCHE - females of the species, women-in-progress, unfolding heroines - we band of sisters.

I remember reading early on, among other rebellious stuff, *The Natural Superiority of Women* (written by a man, but hey, I'll take what ya got), Simone de Beauvoir's *Le Deuxième Sexe*, and dogmatic essays telling us the only "right" orgasm for women was vaginal. (*The Myth of the Vaginal Orgasm* was not published until 1970. Who knew?) I was gently and naturally politicized, as organically part of my education at GHS as memorizing Keats, dissecting frogs and learning the Four Causes of the 100 Years War. I remember thinking in my freshman year at college when everybody was talking about the "new" feminism and women's solidarity: "Duh!"

And of course, the most impressive and impression-making of all: Frankie Rubinstein. But she deserves her own tribute.

Loved being Managing Editor of Calliope, loved writing prose and poetry for Mrs. Grossman's Creative Writing class, loved being beaten by Ruth Daly in the chess club, loved somersaulting in Contest. Especially loved cutting any class with Kate. Quite liked French and Italian, although, hell, if GHS can't provide good language instruction, who can? And they sure didn't. But linguistic seeds were planted – and even if you mangled the language, you got to glimpse and read really weird, exotic people.

After freshman year at college where I felt like an alien, I scooped up another three summer months in France. One more painful sophomore year in that mid-western hick college Purdue (my father wanted me to be an aeronautical engineer), where my roommate told me her daddy picked off crows with his shotgun and once asked me, "Who was it who wrote *West Side Story* again? Leonard and Bernstein?" Ouch.

Indiana a bigger culture shock than Europe had ever been. Someone asked me once if I was "a Jewish". They had never seen one. In spite of all my atheistic leanings and religion-shunning, I had to admit, "Yep, I reckon I be one."

Desperate to get out of there to someplace I could breathe, I hightailed it back to France for my junior year abroad. Managed to then test out of my entire college senior year remotely from France, so no need to ever go back to the heart of America, the crossroads of the Bible Belt and the Corn Belt. (Now Trump country. Why am I not shocked?) Pocketed the B.A. and... see ya!

Over the next 50 years, never made it home again for more than a coupla weeks. Master's from University of Strasbourg in France and then skipped across the border to Germany. University instructor at 23, PhD in Linguistics to follow, which gradually allowed me a broadened professional field to leave academics and stoke even further the peripatetic *Fernweh* still bubbling inside me. OK, here ya get the elevator pitch. For the last 30 years I've been dubbing movies: translating and adapting the script, casting and directing the foreign actors, and sound-mixing for American blockbusters in five languages and six countries. Barcelona is now home base. (Home base: where you run to after rounding third. Sorry, it's a reflex - always gotta explain to all the baseball-illiterates who surround me. When doing the dubbed version of *A League of Their Own*, the Parisian actress playing Madonna's character asked me if the pitcher and catcher were on opposite teams. Jeez. France just has zero culture.)

It was our 40th reunion that aroused what I wasn't even aware was also simmering under the surface: *Heimweh*. (See above.) Nobody I knew in Europe shared my past in any way: Broad and Olney? Never heard of it. Phillies? Who huh? Motown? Mo-what? Billy Penn's scroll-in-hand erection on top of City Hall? Pardon me?! Loved having all that European exoticism to bathe in, but wouldn't it be nice to have somebody know what a hoagie was or how to dance the Cool Jerk? I was cut off from my past and everyone who shared it with me. I once taught a class where we read an article that mentioned the name Bob Dylan. The class looked blank. I asked, incredulous, "Anybody heard of him?" One lone student, "Didn't he play the guitar or something?" Me: "Um, yes. Or something."

Right before our 40th, my overly generous and inside-my-head sister (GHS class of 211) suggested innocently that I could have a few friends for dinner at her house the weekend of the reunion. Feel free to invite three or four girls, she extravagantly offered. A few hours later, me: Can it be six? A few more hours later, me again: Can we make it ten? A few hours even later: Can I ask 20 people? The next day: Let's make it an even 27. I don't remember how many I ended up inviting - with my sister adding leaves to the table, pulling out a whole 'nuther table, practically opening up a new wing of her house - I only remember that I hadn't been in touch with 95 percent of the women I invited, just remembered liking them or admiring them for some reason - from close or afar. I think half of them didn't even remember who I was.

We started group emails and, yup, I was hooked again - this time to a bunch of fascinating, passionate, variegated, accomplished, heart-felt, authentic, articulate (ok, loud-mouthed) women who one after the other, I delighted in and felt a kinship with. It hasn't stopped. And the new friendships with women I barely knew make it all the more joyful. Where was Roz Kricheff in my life then? How come I didn't hang with Robin Thomas? What was I doing without Gloria London? And how come I wasn't privy to Susan Dukow's painting pep talks and cooking coaxing? When I tell my later-acquired friends about you all, I find myself sounding like a frickin' cheerleader. Yay for our team, baby! Can't beat us! Gimme a G, gimme an H, gimme an S!

One heady, enriching outgrowth is that over the last dozen years almost a dozen fabulous women have made their way to Barcelona. Can you imagine the thrill? Finally, home comes to visit me at home. I cannot feel more affinity for anyone. Don't underestimate a shared past: these women have slouched along the pink marble halls with their bookbags dragging around their ankles, have put up with Dr. Thompson's prig-giness, have snuck a ciggy-butt in the bathrooms, have confided who they went to second base with, have been instilled insubordination by

Frankie, have endured the gym suits, have sung "her glory be our pride", … have… have … have all these things. And I have, too! (Second base: where the cut-off man to the centerfielder stands and is allowed to touch your boobs.)

And now coronavirus creeps into our lives. Even more tightening of the unity - the Zooming in on each other's lives, the sharing of both current and past experiences. I want to hear it all. I never tire of it. Ok, ok - once I fell asleep on a Zoom - but it was two a.m. for me out here in the jungle. What woke me was everyone screaming at the top of their lungs, "Caaaandy! You are so busted!" What greater gesture of love can any girl expect from her friends?

Best of all, the scanning glance over a computer screen of 36 women in front of me and 56 years behind me. What, you felt inferior academically? What, you felt you didn't fit in? What, you couldn't give a shit? Yeah, right, tell me about it.

Barcelona, Spain
December 2020

Arlene Suttin Roman, one of Ellen Williams Lebelle's classmates...

... and Lynn Rosen Lampert in Miss Littman's senior French class.

Ellen Williams Lebelle

MARGOT AND MONONCLE
AND HOW THEY BROUGHT ME TO FRANCE

WE ALL HAD A GOOD LAUGH WHEN DISCUSSING THIS writing project. Who had Miss Littman for French? Who had that horrendous experimental audio-visual course?

I don't remember too much about those classes - who was in them with me. I remember Barbara Ninos was there. She has been a constant friend all these years, one of the band/orchestra group. And others were there. For some reason, I took pictures in that class our senior year. I guess that shows how much I concentrated on learning French. After two years of that experimental course, a different teacher in 11th grade tried a more traditional approach and in 12th grade, it looks like Miss Littman was continuing on that path. The damage, however, was already done.

Our experimental course starred Margot and Mononcle. I write "mononcle" as one word because I thought that was his name. It took me a long time to realize it was "mon oncle". Margot was travelling to France with her uncle! I thought he was just some old man named Mononcle. I thought it was strange, but I didn't think too much about it.

I remember scenes. They checked into a hotel. They visited Mont St. Michel and I think they had an omelet at La Mère Poulard, but that might have been some other vision. Looking at Mont St. Michel, there was a scene with sheep in the meadow and whitecaps on the sea and both were called "moutons". That is the only vocabulary I remember. They visited Chambord and I learned that the salamander was the mascot for François I.

When I got to Pitzer College I wanted to study Spanish but they made me take a proficiency test to make sure I met the four years of high school French qualification, and I failed. That meant I had to take a grammar class. The teacher was Jacqueline Martin and all of sudden, at last, it clicked. The next semester I took a conversation class with Claude de Cherisey, a literature class (the existentialists!) with Jacqueline Martin and another course on music and literature with M. Kardos (good class, but creepy guy).

Claude de Cherisey's visa was expiring and it was not renewed. She could not remain at Pitzer so the school created its first study abroad program for Spring semester 1970. Unlike most study abroad programs at the time, it was not limited to juniors; it was not a year abroad; and it was not just for French majors. I was accepted and came to France the first time as a sophomore in Spring semester. There were thirteen of us, I think. Some chose to live with families; a few were able to live in Claude's apartment. A few of us chose to live at a hotel on Bd. St. Germain, next to the engineering school Eyrolles. Many students from the engineering school, the nearby medical school, and the Sorbonne lived there. One of those students was Paul.

So, there you have it. From a lousy French class in high school which led me to fail a proficiency test on arriving at college I ended up majoring in French and marrying a Frenchman and living in France. Claude de Cherisey remained a good friend until she died. When she took our group on a two-week trip to Normandy, Brittany, and the Loire valley during Easter break 1970, we went to Mont St. Michel and I remembered the "moutons" and when we visited Chambord, I remembered the significance of the salamander.

And how that brings me to you, my 212 classmates.

For me, I've just met you. I don't remember you from high school. For a long time, only some old high school friends came over and got in touch with me: Barbara, Erica (Zissman), Gail (Berlin). They have been my close friends. We did not go to the 40th reunion in 2008. I already had my trip scheduled for the summer to finish off my mother's estate with my brother and could not schedule another for October. However, Erica organized a weekend in the Catskills, not far from where Gail was doing a Balkan folk camp. Barbara and Mike made a trip to Boston to visit Erica and Morty and then drive down with them. I drove in from Pittsburgh. Bonnie and Joan also came. This was the band/orchestra group. It was lovely. It was our lovely mini-reunion and it gave me my first inkling for more.

I don't know how I found out about the email list, but I got on to that and then that morphed into the Facebook group. After the 40th reunion, though, you started coming over and looking me up. I love spending time with you. There were some really interesting, serious discussions in the email group; on Facebook, they tend to be shorter and less profound. That's how I met you and I said to myself what a good group of women we are. I managed to convince Erica to come to the 45th reunion and that is when I met so many of you wonderful women in person. That spawned the idea of a reunion in Paris, which we did in 2015. And I convinced Gail to come to the 50th reunion. By this time, I had so many friends from high school, so many more than I ever did in the '60s.

For us, this year would not have been an important reunion year. We are lucky in that. We have been blessed with Zoom and WhatsApp! Borders and time zones hardly matter. All it takes is for one of us (me, in this case) to say how horrible French was, for another (Gloria) to ask if I had Miss Littman, and a burst of laughter to unite us.

Paula Glenn Lamb has written to me to say that she also went through Margot and Mon Oncle with Miss Littman, maybe in class with me. She also suffered through it and survived. We at Girls' High were not alone. She sent me a link to this blog: https://charliebarnett.com/blog/return-mon-oncle/

Paris, France
December 2020
https://ellenlebelle.blogspot.com/?m=1

Judy Wong Greco

CHOP SUEY
SAME, SAME, BUT DIFFERENT

FROM THE TIME I WAS A LITTLE GIRL, I WAS TAUGHT BY my parents to blend in, to not bring attention to myself, and above all else, "DON'T BRING SHAME TO THE FAMILY" meaning my immediate family and also all Chinese Americans. (We are the "Model Minority" for a reason.) They did name me Judy, after all... Judy not Judith. Why give me a name that they weren't going to call me and also, there is no "th" sound in the Chinese language. When I was born, Judy was one of the most popular and common girl names. I also have a Chinese name which is not noted on my birth certificate but what my family called me. My Chinese name is Tienyan which means Heavenly Sparrow. My family called me Tienyan or Yan at home and Judy outside the home. My parents also did not want me to suffer from being teased for having a Chinese name. Oh, if they only knew. A boy in first grade called me Judy Booty. So much for not being teased, but at least I wasn't teased for being Chinese.

Chinese is my first language because my parents wanted my older brother and me to be able to talk to my grandparents. My parents' line of thinking was that we would learn how to speak English in school. I spent the first three years of my life in Chinatown, San Francisco. We moved to Seattle when I was three years old and what a culture shock that was for me! We went from a crowded dingy apartment building in Chinatown with people who looked like me to literally a white house with a white picket fence and all white people!

It was time to assimilate and start blending in. We were leaving Chinatown behind for a better life. But, not so fast. I was about to draw attention to myself and bring shame to my family.

I developed a stutter in first grade and I could not pronounce the "th" sound. I was in the lowest reading group. My parents were called to school for a meeting about me! The teacher wanted to put me in a special class... special education!!! Here I was, bringing shame to the family at an early age! My older brother was just breezing through school, but not me! Shame! I decided that it was better to just hang my head and not say anything, rather than stutter! Thank goodness that the Special Education teacher was understanding, kind and patient and was willing to work with me. Two months later, another meeting was called with my parents. I was able to pronounce the "th" sound... progress. She also explained to my first-grade teacher and my parents why I was stuttering. I was thinking in both Chinese and English and my thought process was going faster than I could say the words. As a result, I would get frustrated and start stuttering. She told my teacher and parents to give me time to form my thoughts and give me time to speak, to not rush me. She told them that I was actually very bright and did not belong in Special Education. Wow, someone that believed in me and advocated for me. Shame averted! I did move up to the top reading group by the end of the year. No, my parents did not praise me for moving up to the top reading group because it was an expectation. Every once in a while, I will still feel myself begin to stutter and I will just take a deep breath and gather my thoughts and start over.

Fast forward to my sophomore year at Girls' High... I was doing a pretty good job of blending in and not calling attention to myself... just enough for my parents to not get called to a parent meeting. Yes, I was literally scared straight from my experience in first grade. I never wanted to bring shame to my family.

I loved to dance and I was in Dance Concert. My Dance Concert teacher encouraged me to choreograph a dance for our Sophomore Dance for Contest. I was thrilled beyond measure. The day came for me to perform my number for the tryout. There were the PE teachers...

and my Dance Concert teacher smiling at me, giving me an encouraging look. I was in a black leotard with my long black hair pulled back into a ponytail. The music was put on and I started dancing... Stop!!! My Dance Concert teacher had this shocked look on her face as one of the PE teachers went over to the record player to stop the music. I remember that she scratched my 45-rpm record. She said that the song was much too racy and lewd and where did I learn to dance like that; did my parents know that I listened to that kind of music and if they didn't know, they were going to know now when they met with Dr. Thompson! The song was "What's New Pussycat" by Tom Jones. (I actually thought it was a pretty good dance with leaps, splits, and spins... and a few slithers and come hithers. We ended up doing a hula dance dressed in mumus to "Little Brown Gal" with a lot of gyrating hips!) I am sitting in Biology class a few days later when I heard, "Judy Wong, report to the front office." Of all classes to be called out of, I had to be called out of the meanest and most judgmental teacher's class. She definitely gave me the evil eye when I walked out of class. Yep, there were BOTH of my parents with Dr. Thompson. My parents did not understand why they were called to the meeting, that I was a good girl and that I had good grades. Dr. Thompson explained the situation to them about my suggestive and lewd dancing to inappropriate music, and that they needed to talk to me. My father asked if I had cheated in class. Dr. Thompson said that was not why they were called in, that I was not cheating. My father asked if I had talked back to a teacher. Dr. Thompson again said no, that was not why they were called in. At this point, I could see my parents stiffen up at the same time and give her the phony polite look with the fake smile to rude customers at the restaurant. My father said yes, that he would talk to me when I got home. At this point, I'm thinking I just punched my ticket to Hallahan, the parochial school for good Chinese American girls, oh great, just great. I brought attention to myself and shamed the family!

When I got home from school that day, there were both my parents waiting for me in the living room. My brother was there too. I held my head down making no eye contact ready for my punishment for bringing shame to the family. Yes, my parents had a talk with me, but most likely not the kind of talk that Dr. Thompson thought they were going to have with me. They thought that I had been caught cheating or been disrespectful to a teacher. That would have brought shame to the family. They had seen me practice the dance at home, and they thought it was a good dance to a good song. They did not disagree with Dr. Thompson in her office outwardly, out of respect for her position, but they did give her that look reserved for rude customers. I was stunned! They were actually being supportive of me, albeit not in front of Dr. Thompson. I learned something that day. I learned that my parents were going to support me if they felt I was wronged. They just told me to continue to be a good girl and maybe not dance that way in school.

This was a seminal point in my relationship with my parents and my relationships with my teachers at school. I was not ever going to bring shame to my family. I became more guarded with the teachers at school not revealing anything about my home life, not that there was anything to reveal. I learned about family love and loyalty. Yes, I always knew that my parents loved me, but even more so that day.

Footnote #1: There is a backstory to every backstory to the story. How did I get my nickname Wongstein in high school and how did it evolve to O'Wongstein? I will give you the short version as opposed to the whole megillah (Yiddish for a long-involved story.) Back in the day at Girls' High, we were assigned to homeroom in alphabetical order by last name. With my last name Wong, I was in the homeroom with the last part of the alphabet. A few of the girls' names ended in "Stein". One day we had a substitute teacher and during roll call, I told her my name was Judy Wongstein. Everyone thought it was funny and it just stuck. Fast forward to 2008 when we were planning our fortieth reunion. It was time to update my nickname to O'Wongstein to reflect diversity. That's the short version.

Footnote #2: Yes, I was a special education teacher at Columbine High School from 1987 until I retired in 2002. I did not retire because of the tragedy. I had always planned to retire after thirty years of teaching and do something else. I loved my Columbine Family and Community. I had a great career. I tell people that I had just one bad day. Because I was a special education teacher, I was what they called a primary provider for a certain number of students. I guided them through four years of high school and beyond. I stayed with my freshman class from 1998 to 1999 until they graduated in May, 2002. I remember one of my freshman students from the 2001 to 2002 school year asking why I couldn't stay for them until they graduated. One of my students who was a junior at the time said that if I stayed for everyone, I would never get out of there. This is why I must stop writing now, otherwise I will never stop writing.

Footnote #3: Believe it or not, one of my favorite dishes growing up was chop suey, no, not the kind of "slop" that you get in the Chinese American restaurants. Chop suey means bits and pieces in Chinese. My parents were very frugal people and did not waste anything. On the day before we went to Chinatown to get groceries, we would have chop suey. We would use up whatever vegetables and meat we had left. Chop! Chop! Chop!

With the giant Chinese cleaver and it all went into the sizzling peanut oil with garlic and ginger in the wok and there was a stirred fried meal! It was something different each week and delicious. My dad called it "Shanghai Surprise" because it sounded better than chop suey. One of his favorite jokes was what do Chinese people in China call food? Food, lol! I am sure many of you have heard the Asian expression "Same, Same, But Different", yes, no? Now, I don't want to just blend in. Everyone says how the USA is like a melting pot. I prefer to see us as chop suey, all these wonderful little bits and pieces adding up to something good. Same, Same, But Different…acknowledging, accepting, and celebrating the differences.

Littleton, CO
February 2021

Fran Yeager Bembenek

NOVEMBER 2020

The pandemic is a lonely place. Maybe more for those who are living alone, but I think it's lonely to some extent for everyone. We are all here in our own minds with our own worries running through them. Worries for ourselves – will we get sick, will we survive financially, and what if we lose a loved one? For our loved ones – are they ok, are they going to be able to cope? And worries about what life is going to look like "after". And many of us feel lonely because we miss the company of family and friends who we can no longer see in person. Or, if we do see them, we can no longer hug. Or even come close to. Six feet apart with a mask on just doesn't feel enough sometimes.

Slowly, though, things had started being moved to Zoom. Church services could be viewed. Our book club decided to try it, with great success. Classes became available. Life began to open up a bit.

I often say these days, "Thank God for Zoom". And I do feel that way. If it weren't for the fact that just about every activity in my life has moved to it, I would have nothing to do. Church. Book Club. Craft group. Classes. Exercise. Get togethers with friends. You name it, I'm Zooming it.

This week we will be celebrating the Thanksgiving holiday. And today, the "sermon" portion of my church service wasn't a sermon at all, but a conversation between our two senior ministers about how can we possibly find something to be grateful for with all this going on?

They asked each other the question, what is really hurting you in your life right now? And then, they asked the second question – and what are you able to be grateful for in that circumstance?

One missed her father, who is elderly and lives out of state. She can't visit. Can't see him. But, she said, she is grateful for her wonderful, supportive dad, and grateful she can call him every day. And for those of us who no longer have our dads here, yes, that certainly is something to have gratitude for. Puts it into perspective for us.

And while I can't spend time with my friends or go out to activities I normally would right now, I am very grateful for friendships, old and new. And for renewed connection with my 212 sisters as we all reach the seven decades on earth mark. It is one of those blessings that has come along with the pandemic. The stuff that you have to admit you would have not had otherwise.

DECEMBER 18, 2020

I have put this down for almost a month. Another month here in pandemic-land, and watching things just get worse out there in the world. And missing the people I love. But I am still, very, very grateful for the connections I have, especially the ones that go back for years.

I loved my years at Girls' High. I was one of the kids, I have since come to learn, who didn't have it very easy at home. Funny how we all thought everyone else's life was "normal" and we were the only one with issues. School was a refuge for me. My friends were everything to me. Between school and my friends, I had a safe place, I had a life.

But I lost touch with most of the girls after I left school. I graduated, got married, and moved to Texas, where my new husband was in the Air Force. I stayed in touch with a few girls for a few years as we moved around the country. But life got complicated, as it does. My husband was killed in an accident six years later. My life fell apart for a long while after that. And I pretty much lost touch with everyone I had been friends with as I started trying to rebuild a life of my own. And for many years, I left that part of me behind. But… I always had that identity of being a Girls' High Girl. I was always proud of that. To me, those years were what made me who I was in some way I can't define. It was always part of me.

Fast forward forty years. I got a call one night out of the blue from one of my classmates. She had tracked me down despite many moves, name changes, and no longer having anyone left in my family that could have told her where I was. I was so happy to be "found". So happy to hear from her, even though she and I had not been friends in school. We had a few classes together, and I had not heard her name in forty years. And I was so very happy! I felt like I had lost "home" somewhere along the way, but it had reached out and found me again.

I didn't go to the reunion though. I was once again living here in Texas, where I have lived since 1980. Texas is a long way from Philadelphia, and with no one in the area to visit, it was not in the cards to travel to Philly for the reunion. I was happy to know there was going to be one, and did manage to get back in touch with a few friends whom I had lost track of because of it. But going back home was out of the question. So, I missed the 40th, and the 45th, and the 50th.

And here we were suddenly in the pandemic this year, fifty-two years down the road from our graduation day. And living in a very strange new world indeed.

The pandemic took away my job. I worked a seasonal job for the last five years, working with Medicare recipients to help them find insurance solutions. Six months on, six months off. Just at the time I would have been preparing to go back to work, the company shut down to "returners". And my normal "six months off" activities were suddenly shut down when we all had to go into lockdown. No days with friends. No church. No volunteer work. No book club. No yarn club. All gone. Alone, stuck at home and waiting for someone to say it was safe to go out into the world again. Nine months later, we still don't have that word and don't know when it will happen. And we wait, and wait.

FEBRUARY 2021
And we are still waiting… and it looks like it will be a long time, yet, even with the vaccine. (I have received my first shot and am awaiting the

second now.) But we will still be masked and distanced for a long time. But we have had a lot of good things come of this time, as well.

When I heard from the "212 Sisters" that we were going to have a "ReZOOMion", I was over the moon! Finally getting to attend a reunion of my old friends and would not have to travel to do this… and we have been meeting at least monthly lately, and talking to each other, and it has been a wonderful thing. A true gift.

We have reconnected old friendships. We have made new ones with the women we only knew as classmates in passing so many years ago. We are getting to know each other again. And it is a group of awesome women. And I do mean that in the literal sense. I am in awe of so many of my friends.

And I feel like I have gained another gift from my sisters. I have regained a lost part of my life that was misplaced and left behind many years ago. I am finally able to be honest about how hard it was back when I was young. And through that I have regained my real self, that young girl who I was. And friends have been wonderfully supportive in the present moment too, with cards and gifts and "returning" a lost cookbook to me that was discarded in 1970 and missed all these many years! And I am so grateful to all for the talks, the friendship, the support that I feel. I have no way to say thank you enough! (And you know who you are ladies!).

It will be interesting to see our post-pandemic lives and what the world becomes, I know… And, God willing, we will all still be walking through this together for a long time to come.

Mesquite, TX
February 2021
frannieb719@aol.com

Janet Yassen

VALENTINE'S DAY;
FEBRUARY 14, 2021

DEDICATION:

These reflections are inspired by a group of awesome GHS 212 women whose spirits took root at a tender time in all of our lives; and with much gratitude to the love and stewardship that has blossomed from an unanticipated pandemic. NB: Driving from Boston to Atlanta and being on a Zoom call (without video) with 212ers brought more gratitude. I now attribute some of my courage to make this trek to each of you as my sisters in my journey for feminism and to creating a more just society. I didn't know it then and I am so glad to have these reflections unfold over the past 50 years. What a gift to get to re-know many of you and to also meet new classmates at 70. Back to the future while looking through the lens of the past and the mirror of the present.

DISAPPEARED

Many of you may never have known Sandy, who was in our 212 class for a short time. She was a beloved friend from my West Oak Lane neighborhood with whom I shared a locker, near that dreaded stairway that Sherrie climbed for the last time.

Even now, I can feel the leather (or was it vinyl?) of the seats of the booth that we occupied every morning for breakfast at the Esquire Diner with Sandy, Susan and others who unfortunately have receded in my mind (please come forward). Traumatic memory has a way of revealing itself through the body.

One day there was no more Sandy ordering eggs and rye toast. Calls to her home went unanswered, until finally her mom told us 'girls' that Sandy "needed a change of scenery, and was in Florida." Girls' High, was in fact a "stressful place," she said. (Facts become hazy over time, but feelings do not.) Sandy's unexpected departure shook our adolescent view of the world in which girlfriends just don't leave without saying good-bye.

We commiserated about what happened to our dear friend and the deep loss that we felt. Our memories have continued vividly as traumatic memories tend to do. Flashes of Sandy riding off after school on the back of her boyfriend's motorcycle, her bright smiles matching her bright hair, her loyal friendship and pillow talks.

The narrative abruptly stops in my brain. Sandy eventually returned, but not to GHS. The content of her stress remained undisclosed to me, especially since I left Philadelphia after Temple University and moved immediately to Boston in my friend M's used but useful car. I have created an incredibly meaningful and grateful life, beyond my own working-class imagination. No regrets, except for missing the roots of my early life, the best soft pretzels on the planet and, of course, my friendship with Sandy that sadly drifted apart. As I write this, I have reunited with my 'grandsuns' (and their parents), who moved to the Atlanta area in August of 2020. Possibly it is serendipity that they live in Sandy Springs, or maybe not. A fitting place to grow my memories of Sandy and GHS and to grow new ones. Good idea for our 70th year.

Although Sandy disappeared twice in my life (one as a shrouded mystery; second from an early death), the pandemic of COVID19, and the connections with GHS 212 women, brought back so many of my memories of Sandy. She will always have a special place in my heart. I wish that I could convey to her my regret that, because of the culture of the time, there were things that were just not talked about. I was robbed of being able to extend my unconditional love and caring to her for whatever she was going through; and my sorrow that she could not be with her buddies from the Esquire Diner. But now I can shout it, and maybe she can hear me. Happy 'Galentine's' day, my beloved girlfriend.

TALE OF TWO PANDEMICS; BOOKENDS

My mother was one when the flu pandemic
shaped her life a century ago.
From my COVID19 pandemic perch seeing it in rear view;
looking to chat with mom, about what an impact we each now know.

She gave me her resilience, so that I could thrive,
Maybe I gave something to her, to help her to survive??
Deep reflections now so unexpected, and yet...
My long gone mother keeps on giving; her resilience is my net.

We each felt alone in what we had to do
Neither of us knowing how to get through.
With viruses invisible, our new bond was formed.
Keep moving forward; through roses and through thorns.

Rage creates an energy of force,
Mom, do not mistrust kindness, also a life giving source.

As Amanda Gorman exalted; You were not really broken.
Just unfinished tasks, your legacy has spoken.

I humbly took on this mission without either of us knowing,
Thanks for the challenge to keep on growing.

You were just a baby looking for secure love,
Now both pandemics connect us, yours from above.

It's okay that you never understood me,
though you tried from time to time.
However, your unwavering love taught me how to rhyme!

Newton, MA
February 2021